Paths and Grounds of Guhyasamaja According to Arya Nagarjuna

(With Commentary by Geshe Losang Tsephel)

Master Yangchen Gawai Lodoe

Translated
by
Tenzin Dorjee
(co-translator on root text Jeremy Russell)

Edited by
David Ross Komito and Andrew Fagan

LIBRARY OF TIBETAN WORKS AND ARCHIVES

ISBN: 81-85102-94-5

Published by the Library of Tibetan Works and Archives, Dharamsala, H. P. (India) and printed at Indraprastha Press (CBT), 4 Bahadurshah Zafar Marg, New Delhi 110002.

Dedication

Even though the self and others
Equally wish for happiness but not suffering;
Since others are more important
May altruism to establish all in happiness
Spread universally in the hearts
Of all sentient beings pervading space.

His Holiness the Dalai Lama of Tibet, the 1989 Nobel Laureate.

I dedicate this humble yet significant book to all of my great spiritual masters, above all to His Holiness the Dalai Lama, who have shown me infinite loving kindness and care and transmitted priceless teachings. May they live for ages to come and may all mother sentient beings always come under their compassionate care and enlightened guidance.

Acknowledgement

I have been helped by many people in presenting this book to the empowered minds and the receptive eyes. I am grateful to them all but my special thanks are due to: my kind masters Venerable Geshe Lobsang Tsephel for his commentary; Venerable Geshe Sonam Rinchen (especially for his valuable teachings at the Library for twelve years while I served as his translator) and Venerable Geshe Dawa for their helpful clarifications; my translation colleague Jeremy Russell and his wife Philippa Russell for their class notes; Dr. Andrew Fagan for his editorial help even during his busy schedule at the Delek Hospital, and my old friend Professor David Komito for re-editing the complete manuscript even during his Yamantaka retreat in Dharamsala; Mr. Gyatsho Tshering, our director, for his trust, friendship and inspiration during my twelve years' service in the Translation Bureau of the Library of Tibetan Works and Archives, and to my colleagues Tenzin Choedon, Tsering Norzom and Pasang Chozom for their help in preliminary typing.

Publisher's Note

In many Tantras and works of highly realised masters, Guhyasamaja is described as 'the supreme and king of all Tantras'. Thus we are extremely pleased to publish this edition of *The Paths and Grounds of Guhyasamaja According to Arya Nagarjuna*. Guhyasamaja is studied and practised in all the traditions of Tibetan Buddhism, with the Gelugpa tradition placing particular emphasis upon it. It is an essential part of Highest Yoga Tantra, and studying it undoubtedly facilitates understanding of other Tantras of the same class.

The text presented here is selected from *Yangchen Galo's Paths and Grounds of Tantra*. Yangchen Galo was a saint-scholar in 18th century Tibet who belonged to the Gelugpa tradition. The commentary is provided by Venerable Geshe Lobsang Tsephel who presented this text in Buddhist philosophy classes at the Library of Tibetan Works and Archives in Dharamsala, in 1986. Mr Tenzin Dorjee Lotsawa was his accomplished translator and subsequently devoted himself to producing the work in book form, with the assistance of Jeremy Russell. We are grateful to Geshe Lobsang Tsephel, and to the translator and editors, for their dedicated efforts to make the Guhyasamaja Tantra accessible to serious practitioners of Tibetan Buddhist Tantra.

It should be noted that Tantra is a swift but risky path to enlightenment. It is extremely profound, is codified in a special terminology, and is dependent upon the explanation, advice and personal guidance of a qualified teacher. We therefore strongly advise that only practitioners who have received the Guhyasamaja Empowerment or an empowerment into another Highest Yoga Tantra should make use of this book.

It is our sincere hope that this work will be of inestimable benefit to students of Highest Yoga Tantra and, through them, will contribute to the welfare of all sentient beings.

Gyatsho Tshering
Director   April, 1995

Geshey Losang Tsephel

Contents

Introduction

BACKGROUND

India, the Land of Aryas, gave birth to Buddhism in the sixth century BC. In subsequent centuries the great Tibetan Dharma kings and Lotsawas (translators), the eyes of our world, brought it across the mighty ranges of the Himalayas to the Snow Land of Tibet, the home of Dalai Lamas; thanks to their love and direction, selfless sacrifices and dedication to Buddhism, and also to the great Indian masters who taught the Dharma to Tibetans in India and Tibet. Interestingly, there were prophecies already made by the Buddha and other realized masters with regard to the flourishing of Buddhism in the Snow Land of Tibet. Since the seventh century, Tibet and her people have dedicated basically everything—their resources, time, energy and even their lives - to Buddhism, much as many other countries dedicated everything to materialism. Buddhism has thus deeply penetrated into the minds and blood of Tibetans, so much so that it has become their 'unique identity'. (See *Generous Wisdom by His Holiness the Dalai Lama*, translated by Tenzin Dorjee and edited by Dexter Roberts, published by LTWA, Dharmsala, H.P., pp 1 and 39, 1992). It has in fact overtaken even their indigenous Bon religion. It is now somewhat unthinkable that there could be a Tibetan identity without Buddhism.

The vastness and profundity of Buddhism can be understood from the rich collection of Tibetan Kangyur (Sutras) and Tengyur (Shastras) from the Indian Buddhist tradition, which runs into hundreds of voluminous scriptures, and from the subject matter of these scriptures. Over the centuries Tibetan masters have also penned thousands of works on Buddhism. Within their 'Collected Works' (gsung 'bum) is a class of works known as 'Sa Lam' or 'Paths and Grounds'. These works focus on the structure of paths and spiritual grounds leading to 'Liberation' (thar pa) and 'Enlightenment' (thams cad mkyen pa'i go 'phang) for the sake of all sentient beings, and deal comprehensively with these paths and grounds.

THE TWO VEHICLES

In Buddhism there are two Vehicles: the Vehicle of Seniors (this is the translation of the term 'Theravaddin' which I prefer to the controversial term 'Hinayana' which means the Lesser Vehicle) and the Vehicle of Bodhisattvas. We find in both a complete structure of paths leading to the respective spiritual goals. However, the former vehicle presents only these five paths: the path of accumulation, the path of preparation, the path of seeing, the path of meditation and the path of no-more learning. But in the latter vehicle, not only are these five paths and spiritual grounds presented, they have been done so according to both the Perfection and the Tantric Vehicles. The names of the five paths are the same in both the Vehicles of Seniors and Bodhisattvas. Additionally, the Perfection Vehicle and the Tantric Vehicle present ten grounds between the path of seeing and the path of meditation. Many works have been written on these paths which provide an atlas of 'Liberation' (thar pa) and 'Enlightenment' (byang chub), much like an atlas of the world. From the collection of such works is selected here a work popularly known as *Yangchen Galo's Paths and Grounds of Tantra* (*Yangchen Galo'i Nagkyi Salam*).

ABOUT THE AUTHOR AND HIS WORK

Yangchen Gawai Lodoe is often called by his abbreviated name: Yangchen Galo. He was an eminent saint scholar of eighteenth century Tibet. His other name is A kya Yong zin. It seems there is no biography on him. Belonging to the Gelugpa tradition of Tibetan Buddhism, founded by Manjushri Lama Tsongkhapa, this work on the paths and grounds of Guhyasamaja Tantra, as with his other works, is based on the incomparable masterpieces of Lama Tsongkhapa and his heart-like disciples. Lama Guru Dev, a Mongolian Buddhist monk, published *Yangchen Galo's Collected Works* in two volumes of book style in 1971 in New Delhi. His work on the paths and grounds of Mantra is found in the first volume. The complete title of the work is: *An Eloquent Presentation—A Port of Entry for the Fortunate Ones into the Paths and Grounds of Mantra According to the Glorious Guhyasamaja of the Arya (Nagarjuna) Tradition* (*dpal gsang wa 'dus pa 'phags lugs dang mthun pa'i sngags kyi sa lam rnam gzhag legs bshad skal bdzang 'jug ngogs zhes bya wa bzhugs so*).

Notwithstanding its brevity, this work presents lucidly the paths and grounds of Mantra according to Guhyasamaja Tantra. Perhaps for this and other reasons, when His Holiness the Dalai Lama was consulted to finalize a course syllabus for many young monks admitted to his Namgyal Monastery in 1979, His Holiness authorized its inclusion in the syllabus. This work maps out the two stages of Highest Yoga Tantra: the generation stage and the completion stage.

The author presents his work under two major outlines: the mode of progression on the paths and the mode of establishing the ten grounds and the five paths. The former outline contrasts the two stages of Highest Yoga Tantra with the two yogas of the three Lower Tantras and the path of the Perfection Vehicle. He writes conclusively that one must eventually enter the path of Highest Yoga Tantra in order to achieve enlightenment. Khedrup Rinpoche in his *General Exposition of Tantras (mkhas grub rje'i rgyud sde spyi rnam)* states:'Although one can reach the tenth ground by the paths of the Perfection (Vehicle) alone, if one is eventually to attain Buddhahood, one must follow the path of Highest Tantra; otherwise it is impossible to attain Buddhahood.' Also, with the path of Highest Yoga Tantra, unlike the three Lower Tantras, even a new practitioner can attain enlightenment in 'just one lifetime of this degenerate era'. Its two stages are presented under the five outlines as follows: definition, division, etymological explanation, the criteria for having completed the two stages and the mode of transference from a lower level to a higher level. In order to practise the two stages, practitioners must at first receive a complete empowerment according to a standard Tantric source from a qualified spiritual master, continually abide by the tantric vows and commitments and then study well the two stages under his or her guidance. These two stages must be practised in sequence according to the Tantras and their standard commentaries written by great realized masters. In other words, one cannot practise them out of the prescribed order. The *Five Levels (rim lnga)* states:

'For those who abide well on the generation stage
And wish for the completion stage,
Buddha has presented these ways (the two stages)
Just like the rungs in a ladder.'

In light of this, Yangchen Galo's work on the paths and grounds is a valuable aid to one's meditational practice.

The second major outline explains the five paths and ten grounds according to the two vehicles: the Perfection and the Tantra. Having consulted numerous sources, our author writes that as far as the names of the grounds are concerned some sources have the same names for the grounds in Tantra as in the Perfection Vehicle but others have different names. In regard to the number of grounds, the Perfection Vehicle asserts ten to eleven grounds at the most but in Tantra the grounds are listed from eleven to even sixteen according to various sources. However, the grounds of the Perfection Vehicle and those of Tantra are correlated and the author emphatically states that the differing number of grounds between the two vehicles and also within the Tantric Vehicle is just a matter of classification. Thus, there is no contradiction. Conclusively speaking, all the grounds are included within the five paths. These paths can be likened to our modern highways with their route numbers and travelling on them is safe, enjoyable and above all enlightening. As long as practitioners keep themselves on these paths there is no chance of going astray.

The Teaching and the Translation at the LTWA

In 1986 Venerable Geshe Lobsang Tsephel of the Jangtse College of Gaden Monastic University taught *Yangchen Galo's Paths and Grounds of Mantra* in his regular classes at LTWA. Previously, he had taught at the Namgyal Monastery for several years. At present, he is based at his Dharma center in San Diego, CA, and also teaches at other Dharma centers in the United States as a Visiting Geshe. Before giving this teaching, at the very outset he announced that if possible those who wished to attend the course should have received a Guhyasamaja Empowerment or an empowerment into any other Highest Yoga Tantra. The uninitiated were advised not to attend the course. His teaching method was simple and direct. I translated for him and also recorded his commentary for the library. My friends Jeremy Russell and his wife Philippa Russell took notes of his commentary at the time. Later, Jeremy and I translated the original work of *Yangchen Galo's Paths and Grounds of Mantra* into English and also restored Geshe la's commentary on it from the notes and tapes of the course. We have faithfully translated the text with the minimum interpolation of words (given in parenthesis) as contextual clarifiers. We have not taken much liberty with the text while rendering it into English. This has been our uncompromising translation policy even when readability suffers occasionally. Above all, we did this in order to prevent faults of omission and commission in the main text. Preserving the originality to commentators may also give different but standard commentaries on the text and the readers are not obligated to accept just one commentarial interpretation. Readers may find it difficult to follow the translation at times because of the technical nature of the work translated herein. Nonetheless, we trust that initiated and enthusiastic readers will surely face the challenge. At our Translation Bureau we have been keeping alive the spirit of team work that had been started by the great Indian masters and Tibetan Lotsawas (Eyes of the World) in ancient Tibet. We are convinced that this ensures a qualitative and readable translation of Buddhist literature. From 1981 to 1990 my main focus has been translating relentlessly for the regular Dharma classes for westerners at the LTWA, and from 1991 to 1993 I have also been asked to teach here and abroad.

After completing our first draft I translated Geshe la's commentary back to him in Tibetan and then edited the manuscript in English accordingly. I also verified our translation of the fundamental text with the original work in Tibetan before leaving for my North American talks and translation tour which took up most of 1991. Returning to the Library, once again I verified our translation with the original work and edited it accordingly. Geshe la's commentary is presented here more or less as he gave it. It throws light on a number of points and includes a major part of the *Sadhana or Liturgy of Guhyasamaja* from the point of view of practice.

For better understanding Jeremy and I decided to merge the fundamental text into Geshe la's commentary. With this in order, the fundamental text is presented in indented form. As for the presentation of his teaching, mostly Geshe la would first read a portion of text and then comment on it. Alternatively, sometimes he would give a commentary first and then sum it up by reading the relevant passage from the text. This style should be remembered while reading this book. In order to facilitate the flow of reading, generally I have avoided as much as possible using Tibetan and Sanskrit terms in my translation; I have mostly given them in parentheses at their first occurrence, juxtaposed to the English terms.

Going through Geshe la's commentary I noticed that from a western scholarly point of view it needed a great deal of reworking. However, considering the esoteric nature of this work and also fearing to recomment on his commentary I have contented myself with providing an introduction, an outline of the Tibetan text, end notes with which to clarify a number of significant points, a bibliography and a list of a few related works in English. This aside, everything else is certainly beyond my humble project. As this book is intended for advanced Tantric practitioners of Highest Yoga Tantra, particularly Guhyasamaja, I have omitted a glossary for they are expected to be familiar with most of the Dharma terms. Notwithstanding any of its failings, I hope this book proves a valuable guide and manual for the intended practitioners.

THE SUPREMACY OF GUHYASAMAJA

In many Tantras and works of realized masters, Guhyasamaja is referred to as 'the supreme and king of all Tantras'. Without relying upon its path there is no way to attain supreme enlightenment. (See Khedrup Rinpoche's *An Ocean of Attainments of the Generation Stage (bskyed rim dngos grub rgya mtsho)*, p 8, in Tibetan). Conclusively speaking, the existence of Guhyasamaja is as much an essential for the survival of Tantras as Vinayapitika (the Basket of Ethics) is for the existence of Buddha's Teaching in general. The following quotes substantiate this point. Khedrup Rinpoche states, 'Whether or not the essence of Buddha's Teaching exists is dependent on whether or not this (Guhyasamaja) exists, it is said,'(Ibid). The *Oral Transmission of Manjushri ('jam dpal zhal lung)* also states, 'It is emphatically stated that the precious Teaching of Buddha exists at a time when this (Guhyasamaja) exists with its meaning transmitted into ears. But, if this lineage is broken everyone should know that Buddha's Teaching has come to an end.' (See Khedrup Rinpoche,Ibid, p 7). Acharya Chandrakirti's *Bright Lamp (sgron gsal)* also states that Guhyasamaja is the pinnacle of all Tantras for it is the source of all other Tantras and the vessel of all Sutras.

HOW GUHYASAMAJA IS KING OF ALL TANTRAS

It is impossible to attain supreme enlightenment without non-dual bliss and emptiness, spontaneously arisen exalted wisdom and the two sets of four joys or bliss (of the sequential and the reverse orders). Also, in order to be enlightened in this life one must accomplish within this life the Complete Enjoyment Body adorned by major and minor marks of the 'state of union with seven features'. But, this body (of ours) precipitated by previous karmic actions and delusions can never become the Complete Enjoyment Body. On the one hand, if one abandons this ordinary body and then achieves the Complete Enjoyment Body in the next rebirth, obviously one has not achieved it in this life. On the other hand if one achieves such a body adorned by major and minor marks in this life by changing the ordinary body then the Complete Enjoyment Body would have arisen without its 'similar type' cause (rigs 'dra'i rgyu). That is impossible too. One must, therefore, understand well from what kind of 'similar type' cause the Complete Enjoyment Body is accomplished, by what sort of antidotes this impure (ordinary) body is abandoned and how the Complete Enjoyment Body is accomplished and then practise the paths. Otherwise, without having even a basis for accomplishing the Complete Enjoyment Body adorned with major and minor marks, if one claims that one will become an enlightened being by actualizing the spontaneously arisen exalted Wisdom Truth Body after having familiarized oneself with a clear, blissful and non-conceptual mind, one has to accept an enlightened person in an ordinary body having just the Truth Body and lacking the Complete Enjoyment Body and the Emanation Body etc. This is absolutely impossible. With regard to how the Complete Enjoyment Body adorned with major and minor marks is accomplished by abandoning this impure (ordinary) body, one must learn about it by pleasing qualified lamas/masters and receiving their pith-instructions (in accordance with) the most extensive explanation of the illusory body in the *Glorious Guhyasamaja Tantra (dpal ldan 'dus pa'i rgyud),* and its clear elucidation by the pith-instructions of Arya Nagarjuna, the spiritual father, and his spiritual sons. Although other Tantras explain extensively the union of bliss and emptiness etc., the way to accomplish the exalted Wisdom Body adorned with major and minor marks in this life by way of abandoning this impure body is very hidden in them and presented inadequately. In this regard, if one definitely ascertains how the *Guhyasamaja Tantra* explicitly and most extensively explains the way in which the Complete Enjoyment Body is accomplished in this life (which is extremely difficult to understand from other Tantras), one will gain unshakable faith in the supremacy of *Guhyasamaja* over all other scriptures and see that there is no path superior to this. (See Khedrup Rinpoche, Ibid, pp 9-10).

GUHYASAMAJA PROVIDES STRUCTURE TO OTHER HIGHEST YOGA TANTRAS

Guhyasamaja is studied and practised in all the traditions of Tibetan Buddhism. However, the Gelugpa tradition puts great emphasis on it just as other traditions emphasize some other Tantras such as Hevajra. His Holiness the Dalai Lama has said that the Guhyasamaja provides structure to other Highest Yoga Tantras and, therefore, studying and familiarizing oneself with it is essential, for it makes it easier to understand and practise other Tantras of the same class. Khedrup Rinpoche in his *Short Writing (yig chung)* says, "Moreover, if one initially understands Guhyasamaja one will automatically (without the need to put forth much effort) understand other (Tantras). But, if (the order) is reversed the benefits will be fewer; therefore, Guhyasamaja is taught first." The *Bright Lamp (sgron gsal)* also states, "This is the supreme subsidiary practice; a compendium of the meanings of all Tantras."

My intention in presenting this book on Guhyasamaja is two-fold: firstly, to ensure the survival of Tantric Buddhism and, secondly, for myself and the other practitioners to generate more and more intimacy with the path of Guhyasamaja leading towards enlightenment. Another important work that Jeremy and I translated from the Tibetan into English is the *Stages of Pure Yoga (rnal 'byor dag rim)* by Lama Tsongkhapa. I translated its commentary for Ven. Geshe Lobsang Tsephel when he gave it at the LTWA during the 1986-1987 session. The *Stages of Pure Yoga* itself in fact is a commentary of the generation stage of Guhyasamaja. His Holiness the Dalai Lama had taught it in 1985 at his Temple here in Dharamsala. LTWA is going to publish our translation for the benefits of the Guhyasamaja practitioners.

A WORD OF CAUTION ON TANTRA

Tantra is as risky a path as it is swift. No matter how profound and swift a path Tantra is, it alone will not lead one to enlightenment without the *three principal paths (lam gtso rnam gsum)* which are: the determined wish to be liberated (nges 'byung), altruistic mind of enlightenment (byang sems) and wisdom that ascertains emptiness (stong nyid rtogs pa'i shes rab). These are explained in the Perfection Vehicle. His Most Eminence Kyab Je Ling Dorjee Chang, the late Senior Tutor to His Holiness the Dalai Lama, has aptly remarked:"Yak butter cheese cake is delicious because of the butter. Otherwise it would be just a dry ball of cheese. Similarly, Tantra is swift and profound because of the Sutras. Otherwise, it would simply be packed with HUM HUM and PHAT PHAT." As a matter of fact, it is not enough for a doctrine to be Highest Yoga Tantra, a practitioner must become a person of Highest Yoga Tantra. And for this it is a must to cultivate *the three principal paths* and the path of Highest Yoga Tantra. Manjushri Lama Tsongkhapa has lucidly and insightfully captured *the three principal paths* in his poem of that name. Tantra cannot be studied and practised at random and haphazardly. I cannot over emphasize the necessity to study and practise *the three principal paths* before entering Tantra.

NEED FOR A QUALIFIED MASTER

Tantra is extremely profound and is codified in a special terminology. Tantric literature does not present everything explicitly for modern readers. It can be read on many levels for which a qualified master's elucidation is absolutely necessary. The *Five Levels (rim lnga)* states,

> "The technical points have been sealed
> In the Glorious Guhyasamaja Tantra.
> Must learn these from the words of lamas
> Following the way of Explanatory Tantras." (See Khedrup
> Rinpoche, opcit, pp 21-22).

Therefore, it is indispensable to rely upon a qualified spiritual master in order to understand and practise Tantra unmistakably. Dedicated practitioners must cultivate qualified spiritual masters, delight them and request their pith-instructions on Tantra and then practise accordingly. They should not simply feel contented reading Tantric literature on their own. Vajra masters' pith-instructions clarify many hidden points of Tantra and essentialize them for practice. However wonderful a book on Tantra may be, it cannot replace the pith-instructions and experiences of qualified masters. Nonetheless, through this venture of good heart I hope to repay a fraction of the infinite kindness of my spiritual masters and all mother sentient beings.

In conclusion, I would like to state that despite my best intentions and efforts, errors may have slipped into the translation for which I alone am responsible. For all my failings I seek forgiveness from: my incomparable spiritual masters, meditational deities, Buddhas and Bodhisattvas, Viras and Dakinis, Dharma protectors and protectresses. Last but not least from my Dharma friends as well. Lamenting on how, unfortunately, Tantric literature has today become a market commodity due to our materialistic attitude, I hope this book induces universal faith and understanding of Buddhist Tantra in the hearts of readers and practitioners. May my heartfelt prayers be fulfilled.

Tenzin Dorjee (Lotsawa)
Research and Translation Department
LTWA, Dharmsala,H.P.India

The Paths and Grounds of Guhyasamaja According to Arya Nagarjuna

An Eloquent Presentation for the Fortunate Ones to Enter the Paths and Grounds of Mantra According to the Glorious Guhyasamaja of the Arya (Nagarjuna) Tradition.[1]

Part One:
An Introductory and Preliminary Discourse:

A STRUCTURE OF THE PATHS IN BUDDHISM:

Buddhism is universally known as the Teaching of the historical Buddha Shakyamuni who lived in the 6th century B.C. He was a very skillful teacher, teaching something of relevance to all the needs, inclinations and capacities. Therefore, his teaching is vast and profound. Broadly speaking, it is classified into two major vehicles: the Lesser Vehicle and the Greater Vehicle. The former is further classified into two: the Hearers' Vehicle and the Solitary Realizers' Vehicle. Similarly, the Greater Vehicle is also classified into two: the Perfection Vehicle and the Tantric or Vajra Vehicle.[2] In order to attain the remarkable qualities of Buddha's body, speech and mind, we should study and practise the paths and grounds of the Perfection Vehicle and also the exclusive paths of Highest Yoga Tantra.

The Perfection Vehicle exclusively presents five paths and ten to eleven grounds leading to supreme enlightenment. It is the state free of all defilements with their imprints and is also blossomed with all realizations. The five paths are the path of accumulation, the path of preparation, the path of seeing, the path of meditation and the path of no-more learning. The ten grounds are from the Very Joyous to the Cloud of Dharma. These occur between the path of seeing and the path of meditation. There are many texts dealing with the paths and grounds of the Perfection Vehicle such as the one by Khedrup Rinpoche that I taught here at the Tibetan Library in 1985. You may have received similar teachings from other teachers as well. Assuming you have familiarity with the paths and grounds of the Perfection Vehicle, I shall now present the paths and grounds of Highest Yoga Tantra according to Guhyasamaja Tantra.

Generally speaking, Buddhist Tantra is classified into four classes: Action Tantra, Performance Tantra, Yoga Tantra and Highest Yoga Tantra. These are not all different vehicles but constitute just one vehicle, i.e., the Vajra Vehicle. All of them have 'deity yoga' (lha'i rnal 'byor) and also have the same object of intent, i.e. supreme enlightenment. These four classes of Tantra are presented from the perspective of the differing mental aptitudes and capacities of the four main trainees of the Vajra Vehicle in utilizing desire in the path.[3]

Therefore, many tantric sources such as *Samputa Tantra, Hevajra Tantra (kyee rdor gyi rgyud)* and *Ornament of the Vajra Essence Tantra (rdo rje snying po' rgyan gyi rgyud)* differentiate the four classes of Tantras through laughing, looking, embracing or holding hands and entering into union. Briefly speaking, practitioners of these four classes of Tantras are capable of utilizing the bliss derived from those four sensual modes of behavior respectively in the path.

The way the four classes of Tantra are given their names is as follows. Action Tantra is so called because its main trainees resort to many external activities (rather than) the yogas of deity and emptiness. Performance Tantra is so called because its main trainees balance their external activities with internal meditative stabilization. Yoga Tantra is so called because its main trainees primarily cultivate internal yoga rather than resorting more to external activities. Highest Yoga Tantra is so called because its main trainees primarily cultivate a yoga of which there is none higher.

Of the four, Highest Yoga Tantra has its own special features, such as enabling the yogi or meditator to reach supreme enlightenment in just one lifetime of this degenerate era. Highest Yoga Tantra has two divisions: Mother Tantras, such as *Chakrasamvara* ('khor lo bde mchog) and Father Tantras, such as *Guhyasamaja* (gsang wa 'dus pa).[4]

Before starting with this text, which deals with the paths and grounds of Guhyasamaja according to the tradition of Arya Nagarjuna, let me say a word about the place for doing such a practice, who can practise it and how to actually practise it.

Regarding the place, according to the *Twelfth Chapter of the Root Tantra [of Guhyasamaja]* one would accomplish all 'Sidhis' (dngos grub), the attainments in a seclusion in mountains where there are flowers and fruits, etc. Perhaps, the most important features of a place are two: that it should be conducive to our spiritual growth and also if possible where a qualified master of Guhyasamaja is present for consultation and further guidance.

As for the type of person who can practise Guhyasamaja: as with all Tantras, generally speaking, any one with genuine enthusiasm and dedication to Guhyasamaja can practise it after receiving its empowerment from a qualified master. In other words, practitioners must at first receive an appropriate empowerment or empowerment into the class of Tantra that is aspired to be practised. This is particularly important for an empowerment is considered as the entrance to mystical Tantric practice as much as going for refuge in the Three Jewels is so considered for Buddhism generally and the altruistic mind of enlightenment is so considered for Greater Vehicle Buddhism.[5]

THE THREE PRINCIPLE PATHS:

As a matter of fact, one can not jump straight for a tantric empowerment. In order to become the most qualified candidate or practitioner of Tantra, even before going for a Tantric empowerment and practising a particular Tantra, one should have cultivated the three principle paths[6] in one's mindstream. They are the lifeblood of the Greater Vehicle Buddhism. The three principle paths are: renunciation or the determined wish to be liberated (nges 'byung), the altruistic mind of enlightenment (byang chub kyi sems), and the perfect view (yang dag pa'i lta wa), i.e. the wisdom which understands emptiness. Even if one has not actually generated them it would be alright to go for a tantric empowerment if one has familiarity with them based on a sound intellectual understanding. The least qualification needed is to have a genuine enthusiasm and unshakable faith in Tantra as well as the three principle paths.

Briefly speaking, we can generate renunciation by realizing and repeatedly contemplating the general problems and sufferings of cyclic existence and the specific sufferings of its three unfortunate states of rebirths: hell realm, hungry ghosts' realm and animals' realm. We must realize that as long as we wander in cyclic existence, our body and mind are afflicted by a multitude of physical and mental sufferings perpetuated by the three poisonous delusions: ignorance, attachment and hatred. If we realize the extent of true sufferings we will naturally wish to be freed from them.[7] Even as humans, who are much better off than those beings suffering unimaginably in the three lower realms, we suffer at birth, from aging and sicknesses and then at death. Eventually when our life comes to an end, our consciousness will separate from our body; we will experience the agony of death and dying. While wandering in various states of cyclic existence at no time do we experience genuine peace and happiness.[8] Just like an imprisoned criminal who genuinely wishes throughout days and nights to be free from his prison, if we too constantly experience a similar wish, i.e. to be free from cyclic existence, then we have developed a sense of renunciation. From then onwards it should be enhanced by practising appropriate methods.

But, for us to practise Tantra which is extremely profound it is not just enough to have a renunciation. We must also generate great compassion for all other sentient beings. Just as we ourselves are tormented by a multitude of sufferings so too are the other beings who are trapped in cyclic existence. Just as we wish ourselves to be free from sufferings, so too do the other beings. Realizing and repeatedly contemplating the sufferings of other sentient beings in this way, we can experience this kind of compassionate and concerned feeling for others: "How nice it would be if they were freed from their problems and sufferings!" Consider how we ourselves are at present trapped in a problematic situation called samsara or cyclic existence and are thus incapable of liberating others sailing in the same boat. Realizing clearly the situation in which we ourselves are, we will be able to see that only Buddhas or the Completely Enlightened Beings can liberate others by means of their infinite love and compassion, infinite skillful means and omniscient wisdom. Seeing this we should develop Bodhicitta, the altruistic intention to become completely enlightened person for the sake of other sentient beings.[9]

Having generated altruism by examining our own situation and the possibilities of getting out of it, we can see that we are enslaved by delusions. The root of our problems is the innate grasping at self out of ignorance. We misconceive the self as existing separately and objectively from our mental and physical aggregates. It is from this misconception of self that other delusions such as attachment and hatred arise. These delusions cause all kinds of problems for ourselves and others. Therefore, it is very important for us to study and examine the root delusion, i.e. ignorance, and the self grasped at by it.

We have got an innate feeling of a self, as if it exists in and of itself, which does not dependent on anything at all. Some kind of an independent and objective self. Ironically, the self does not exist in this way. There is a disparity between the way in which the self appears to our perception and the way in which it actually exists. We take for granted, as with other phenomena, the existence of the self as it appears to us. In reality, the self, like any other phenomenon, exists dependently.

Every phenomenon for its existence depends on its basis for labelling, its label and a conceptual mind that does its labelling. This realization culminate in direct experience of emptiness: the final mode of the existence of phenomena. This is the ultimate reality—the way in which everything actually exists.[10] .

I do not want to overemphasize the value of the three principle paths. As stated earlier, they are the lifeblood of Buddhism—especially the Greater Vehicle. We should cultivate them for the ultimate benefit of ourselves and others. Even the Tantric Vehicle owes much of its profundity to these three principle paths. For those who genuinely seek enlightenment it is essential to know the paths and grounds of the Perfection Vehicle as well as Tantra. It is within this context that we shall study the paths and grounds of Tantra.

THE TITLE AND THE LINEAGE:

This text which I shall teach you was written by Yangchen Gawai Lodoe (dbyangs can dgah wa' blo gros).[11] Its title in Tibetan is: *Pal Sangwa Duspa Phaglug Dang Thunpai Ngagkyi Salam Namzhag Legshad Kalzang Jugngog Zhesjawa Zhugso (dpal gsang wa 'dus pa 'phags lugs dang mthun pa' sngags kyi sa lam rnam gzhag legs bshad skal bdzang 'jug ngogs zhes bya wa bzhugs so).* In English it reads as follows: *An Eloquent Presentation for the Fortunate Ones to Enter the Paths and Grounds of Mantra According to the Glorious Guhyasamaja of the Arya Tradition.* I have received teachings on the two stages of Guhyasamaja Tantra from His Holiness the Dalai Lama and also from Gaden Tri Rinpoche Zhanphan Nangwa, the 98th throne-holder of Je Rinpoche who is also popularly venerated as Manjushri Lama Tsongkhapa.[12]

As said earlier, we should have received a standard Tantric empowerment to receive teaching on texts such as this. Or at least we should have genuine enthusiasm and a firm faith in the Tantric system. That, I stress upon, as the least qualification to study Tantra. However, without a standard empowerment we can not practise the generation and the completion stages of a Highest Yoga Tantra. I am unequivocal about this. Even if we were to try to practise them on our own we will not achieve any realizations worth their name.

The Glorious Guhyasamaja is presented on three levels: (1) the basis, (2) the path, and (3) the result.

1. On the ordinary level of the basis, the Guhyasamaja could mean the union of the male and female sexual organs. On a subtler level, it is the union of the subtle wind and mind for they are inseparable from each other. This union does not manifest in us in daily situations.[13]

2. On the level of the path, the Guhyasamaja is a union of method and wisdom which is not explained in the Perfection Vehicle and not even in the three Lower Tantras. It is a union of non-dual bliss and emptiness which is exclusively explained in Highest Yoga Tantra.

3. On the level of the result, the Guhyasamaja is the union of the two truths of a non-trainee (an enlightened person). This is not the union of conventional truth and the ultimate truth for it is explained in the Perfection Vehicle as well. But, according to Highest Yoga Tantra this is the union of conventional illusory body and the ultimate clear light.

Concerning the deities of the mandala, according to the Arya Nagarjuna tradition there are thirty-two deities, but according to the tradition of Acharya Jnanapada there are nineteen deities only.

SALUTATION:

Namo Guru Vajradhara.

In accordance with the centuries' old tradition this text also begins with a salutation in Sanskrit: *Namo Guru Vajradhara.* This means,"Homage to the Guru Vajradhara." Vajradhara whose name means a holder of Vajra is the Lord of the Buddhist Tantric Teaching.[14]

AN EXPRESSION OF WORSHIP:

Respectfully I prostrate at the lotus feet
Of the Primordial Protector in the state of union
Who reveals the dance of the rainbow [-like]
Superbly magnificent illusory body with the major and the
    minor signs
From the pure space of simultaneous bliss and emptiness.

This verse contains an 'expression of worship' (mchod brjod). Its temporary purpose is to create positive energy for eliminating mainly external obstacles for the successful completion of the work undertaken and the ultimate purpose of such an expression is to achieve enlightenment for the sake of all sentient beings.

RARITY OF THE HIGHEST YOGA TANTRA:

> Extremely rare to hear for innumerable aeons is even the
>   name
> Of the Highest Yoga Tantra which swiftly bestows
> The state of union with seven features such as embracing
>   each other
> In this short lifespan of the degenerate era.

This verse highlights how the path of Highest Yoga Tantra can take one to the ultimate state of union within this short lifespan of degenerate era. Our's is called a 'degenerate era' (snyigs dus) for it is characterized by strife and violence. The ultimate state of union is characterized by the seven features. The seven features are: complete enjoyment, embracing each other, great bliss, emptiness of inherent existence, compassion, uninterrupted continuum and non-cessation. The verse also reveals the rarity of Highest Yoga Tantra. Shakyamuni Buddha is the fourth in the line of one thousand Buddhas who, according to Greater Vehicle Buddhism, will manifest in our continent within this aeon. Of them all, it is speculated that the eleventh Buddha in the line might teach Tantra as well.[15] And the rest Buddhas will not teach Tantra. This does not at all mean that Tantra is Greek to them but for lack of proper recipients. In this context, it is very rare even to hear the name of Highest Yoga Tantra, let alone finding an opportunity to practise it, for most of the time.

As always, before listening to Dharma teachings it is very important to set up a proper motivation—especially for the study and practice of Greater Vehicle Buddhism and particularly for Tantra such as this. In the present context a proper motivation means an altruistic motivation. We can cultivate it as follows: "I will listen to this Tantric teaching and practise it as much as I can in order to attain enlightenment, fulfilling the wishes all sentient beings have to abandon suffering completely and enjoy genuine, lasting happiness." This kind of motivation is extremely important. If both listener and teacher have such a motivation, that would be most excellent, and our practise would become effective accordingly. Conversely, if we were to lack such an altruistic attitude our practise would not be of much benefit even if the teaching we receive were of the Greater Vehicle, or within that Tantric Vehicle or within that even Highest Yoga Tantra.

A Pledge of Composition:

> Following the incomparable eloquent expositions
> Of Manjunath Tsongkhapa and his spiritual sons
> I shall briefly present in a readable way,
> The mode of progression on the two stages of the path and
>   grounds.

This verse contains the author's 'pledge of composition' (rstom pa dam bca') concerning this text. Its purpose is: for eliminating mainly internal obstacles such as laziness and diversion of interest to some other work, for the successful authoring of this work. Great master Tsongkapa, an emanation of the wisdom deity Manjushri, appeared as a spiritual teacher and composed many monumental works and his way was followed by eminent disciples who also wrote many important works. Our author says that he will follow their remarkable expositions to explain the two stages of the path of Highest Yoga Tantra.

Explaining the Presentation of the Paths and Grounds of Highest Mantra has Two Outlines:

I. *The mode of progression on the paths.*
II. *The mode of establishing the ten grounds, etc., and the 'five paths.*

The former has two sub-outlines:

  A. *General Explanation.*
  B. *Specific Explanation of the mode of progression on the two stages of the Highest (Yoga Tantra).*

I. A. *General Explanation of the mode of progression on the paths:*

A practitioner of Action Tantra attaches more importance to external activities such as bathing thrice a day. But a practitioner of Performance Tantra on the other hand create a balance between his external activities and inner yoga. In sharp contrast to what is said in Action Tantra, practitioners of the Yoga Tantra attach more importance to their inner yoga. The practitioners of Highest Yoga Tantra primarily cultivate yoga that is just unsurpassable. The practitioners of the four classes of Tantra, as said earlier, differ in their faculties and levels of capacity. And this is quite evident if we look at the differences in their mode of behavior and the type of bliss derived thereby which is utilized in their spiritual path.

In Action Tantra, the bliss derived by the partners from gazing at each other is taken as a path. But, these practitioners are not capable of taking other types of bliss such as the bliss derived from embracing each other or the bliss derived from actual union as paths. In Performance Tantra, they derive bliss from smiling and laughing at each other and take it as a path. In Yoga Tantra, the bliss derived from holding hands or embracing each other is taken as a path. In Highest Yoga Tantra, the bliss derived from the two partners entering into actual union is taken as a path.

A number of features such as introducing practitioners to a deity or deities as well as their inestimable mansion, conferring empowerment upon them and keeping their vows and commitments intact are common to all the four classes of Buddhist Tantra. In order to become receptacle vessel of Tantra, all practitioners must first study and practise common paths such as the three principle paths described in *Graded Path (Lamrim)* treatises. And then, they must look for a qualified Vajra master and supplicate him or her to confer a standard Tantric empowerment. For instance, should someone wishes to practise Action Tantra, they should seek to enter its mandala and receive a standard empowerment of a particular deity or deities. This procedure is the same with regard to all the three higher Tantras.

As for mandalas, there are three mandalas common to all classes of Tantra: the colored sand-powder mandala, the cloth or canvas painted mandala and the constructed mandala. Apart from these there are other kinds of mandala such as body mandala, lotus mandala of a consort and the mandala of the ultimate mind of enlightenment.[16] As numerous as mandalas, there are many kinds of empowerment. Empowerment is a rite involving a qualified vajra master conferring an empowerment, a mandala into which one is empowered, ritual substances and implements, offerings and prayers. And more importantly, proper visualization. The master confers empowerment upon a disciple in mandalas. An empowerment is a process by which certain imprints are deposited on one's mindstream to attain realizations and also it empowers one to study, and practise a particular Tantra or Tantras.

EMPOWERMENT IS THE ENTRANCE INTO MYSTICAL TANTRIC PRACTICE.

Generally speaking, there are four types of empowerment: the vase empowerment (bum dbang), the secret empowerment (gsang dbang), the wisdom-knowledge empowerment (shes rab ye shes kyi dbang) and the word empowerment (tshig dbang). The vase empowerment is common to all classes of Tantra but the secret, the wisdom-knowledge and the word empowerment are exclusive to Highest Yoga Tantra. That is because for the study and practice of the generation stage, the vase empowerment alone will do, but the three higher empowerments are needed for the study and practice of the completion stage.[17] Although the three lower Tantras have 'deity yogas' but they do not have the practices of the completion stage. From a numerical point of view, there is a varying number of empowerments from one Tantra to another Tantra. Therefore, it is especially important for the vajra master to know the number of empowerments and the exacting procedure to confer them. The vase empowerment, for instance, is not just a single empowerment but a set of empowerments. While an empowerment is conferred upon it is equally important for a recipient to follow the words of the vajra master[18] and do the visualizations accordingly.

One who has taken any of the seven types of Vows for Individual Emancipation (so thar rigs bdun gyi sdom pa) is a suitable basis for practising Tantra. Alternatively, abiding by the ethics of the ten wholesome actions in general makes a person a suitable basis or a vessel for Tantra. In the two lower Tantras, i.e. Action Tantra and Performance Tantra, only Bodhisattvas' Vows are needed to receive empowerments but in Yoga and Highest Yoga Tantras, in addition to them, one must also take Tantric vows and pledges. If a person abides by any of the seven types of Vows for Individual Emancipation and also Bodhisattvas' Vows and Tantric Vows, he or she will have made the human life most worthwhile and becomes what is known as a 'knowledge holder endowed with the three [sets of vows]' (gsum ldan rig pa 'dzin pa). By virtue of this, he or she has become the best among the practitioners. Above all, one must not breach the vows and commitments which have already been taken, instead should keep them intact as follows. Lest it would be seriously detrimental from spiritual point of view.

If you have received Bodhisattvas' Vows you should see to it that you do not transgress any of the eighteen 'root vows' such as praising oneself and blaming others and the forty six 'secondary vows' such as not teaching Dharma to those who wish to learn it.[19] Similarly, if you have taken the Tantric vows you should not breach the fourteen 'root Tantric vows' such as despising lamas or spiritual masters and the eight 'secondary vows' such as sitting in union without the three recogni-

tions.[20] Keeping our vows and commitments unbreached is as important as receiving them. After taking them it is our prime duty to observe
them. Should we breach any or more of our commitments we must not
stop there; instead, we must purify the breach according to the authentic procedures and practices such as recitation of the hundred syllable
mantra of Vajrasattva and the 'self-empowerment' (bdag 'jug) and
restore them. Either way of purification and restoration is effective.
Self-empowerment in Tantra can be done by those who have completed
a retreat of a deity or deities. Others who have not done such a retreat
can restore their broken commitments through receiving again the
same empowerment from a qualified vajra master or reciting the
Vajrasattva mantra one hundred thousand times with proper visualization.[21]

In brief, in order to engage in Tantric practice we must cultivate the
three principle paths or should have at least a good understanding of
them and an enthusiasm to cultivate them; find a qualified master who
can give us an empowerment and then, keep intact the vows and
commitments after taking them. We should also know well how to
restore them if broken.

THE THREE LOWER TANTRAS, TWO STAGES AND THE PERFECTION VEHICLE:

In the three lower Tantras there is the equivalent yoga with
sign in place of the generation stage and the equivalent yoga
without sign in place of the completion stage. Excepting
these they have neither the concepts of the generation stage
and completion stage nor these terms.

However, these three [lower Tantras] have paths which
accord with the four thorough purities of resultant Buddhahood, an immaculate phenomenon, which can be meditated
upon from right now [the level of the basis]. But, they do not
have paths that can be meditated upon which accord with
the aspects of death, intermediate state and rebirth in [cyclic]
existence, an afflicted phenomenon.

For anything to be either the generation stage or completion stage it should have, right from now, a path [as a
purifier] to be meditated upon which accords with any of the
aspects of the three bases of purification—death, intermediate state or rebirth in cyclic existence and [also any of the
aspects of] the three bodies—Truth Body, Complete Enjoy-

ment Body and Emanation Body—of the purified resultant state of Buddha.

The three lower Tantras do not have the two stages but in place of them they have the 'yoga with sign' (mtshan bcas kyi rnal 'byor) and the 'yoga without sign' (mtshan med kyi rnal 'byor). As for Highest Yoga Tantra, after receiving a complete empowerment, we must practise the two stages: the generation and the completion. Practising these two stages[22] involves meditating on paths which accord with any of the aspects of death, the intermediate state and rebirth, and also any of the aspects of the 'three kayas' or bodies of a Buddha. The lower Tantras do not have such a path but they have paths which accord with the 'four thorough purities of the resultant state' of a Buddha ('bras bu'i yongs dag bzhi dang rnam pa mthun pa'i lam). They are: Abode, Body, Resource and Doctrine.

The Causal Perfection Vehicle and the Resultant Tantric Vehicle are different from each other in many ways. For instance, Bodhisattvas' place of practice is just an ordinary place and they do not generate themselves into a deity. There is no need for them to do so. Neither do they have to purify their environments into inestimable mansions nor bless their resources as in Tantra. But, the Tantric Vehicle does explain the 'four thorough purities of the resultant state' of a Buddha. Practitioners of Tantra should not see their environment as being ordinary but as a pure celestial environment with an inestimable mansion; they have to transform themselves into a deity or deities and hold the divine pride. They transform their resources into the nature of nectar generating blissful experience. Whatever they do such as teaching Dharma they maintain 'the divine appearance' (lha'i gsal snang) and 'the divine pride' (lha'i nga rgyal). The purpose of doing this is to replace an ordinary appearance by divine appearance and an ordinary clinging to 'I' by divine pride. In short, everything is seen as the reflections or the projections of the exalted wisdom of their being a deity or deities.

In the three lower Tantras there is an explanation of generating oneself into a deity or generating a deity in front of oneself, but there is no practice for cultivating paths which accord with any of the aspects of death, the intermediate state and rebirth on the level of basis and taking them into paths. This is a salient feature of Highest Yoga Tantras. In Highest Yoga Tantra it is stated that due to these three ordinary states: death, the intermediate state and rebirth, we find ourselves roaming about in cyclic existence. We, therefore, need a path which accords with their aspects and liberate us from them. By practising the two stages of Highest Yoga Tantra—the generation stage and the completion stage—which contain such a path, we can quickly liberate ourselves from those ordinary states.

THE NEED OF HIGHEST YOGA TANTRA FOR ENLIGHTENMENT:

> The yoga with sign is a deity yoga not conjoined with the wisdom which ascertains emptiness. The yoga without sign is a deity yoga conjoined with the wisdom which ascertains emptiness. One can advance to the tenth ground by the paths exclusive to the Perfection Vehicle and the three lower Tantras but during the final life on the tenth ground one's practice has to be augmented by Highest Yoga Tantra in order to achieve Buddhahood. Without the addition of the path of Highest Yoga Tantra these paths alone will not lead one to Buddhahood. The *Ornament of the Essence—A Commentary to the Wisdom Gone Beyond (phar phyin rnam bshad snying po's rgyan)* says: "The way to accomplish the Form Body by the additional Tantric path, after advancing on the path of the Perfection Vehicle for three countless aeons, should be understood from other [sources]." Also, Khedrup Je's *General Exposition of Tantras (mkhas grub rje' rgyud sde spyi rnam)* says: "Although one can reach the tenth ground by the path of the Perfection [Vehicle] alone, if one is eventually to attain Buddhahood, one must definitely follow the path of Highest Tantra; otherwise it would be impossible to attain Buddhahood."

Should it be said that in such a case it is impossible to attain enlightenment by relying on the paths of the Perfection Vehicle and the three lower Tantras; there is no such fault. One who has reached the tenth ground of the Perfection Vehicle by the respective paths of the Perfection Vehicle and the three lower Tantras achieves Enlightenment in the final life following the additional path of Highest [Yoga Tantra]. It is feasible to assert that he or she has become a Buddha by the paths of the Perfection Vehicle and the three lower Tantras but not by those paths alone. This is so since the Bodhisattva has entered the Tantric path without forsaking the respective paths of those two vehicles. He or she has merely added to them the path of [Highest Yoga] Tantra.

Although the three lower Tantras also accept the attainment of Buddhahood in one lifetime, in their own terms, it is wholly different from the attainment of Buddhahood in one lifetime according to Highest Yoga Tantra. According to those three [lower Tantras], a person of sharp faculties who has completed the yoga without sign accomplishes the feat of long life which lasts for many great aeons. And then relying on the yoga of non-dual clarity and profundity (dzab gsal gnyis med kyi rnal 'byor) he or she ascends the path over a long time in order to achieve Buddhahood. Whereas a distinctive feature of Highest Yoga Tantra is that even if a person has not previously entered the Tantric path and starts out anew that person can achieve Buddhahood during this short lifespan of the degenerate era without taking such a long time.

These two yogas—yoga with sign and yoga without sign—of the three lower Tantras, as stated earlier, are the substitutes (dod) for the two stages of Highest Yoga Tantra. The difference between the two yogas is as follows: a yoga with sign is a deity yoga which is not conjoined with an understanding of emptiness. In contrast, a yoga without sign is a deity yoga which is conjoined with an understanding of emptiness. In other words, the two yogas are distinguished from each other in terms of whether or not they are characterized by the sign of the conception of true existence.

Should the question be raised: Can't a person attain supreme enlightenment by following the individual paths (rang lam) of the Perfection Vehicle and the three lower Tantras? Because at first one reaches the tenth ground of a Bodhisattva by their path, and then engage in the path of Highest Yoga Tantra, which is necessary in order to finally attain supreme enlightenment. Gyaltsab Rinpoche states thus in his work, *Ornament of the Essence—A Commentary to the Wisdom Gone Beyond.* According to him by following the Perfection Vehicle a Bodhisattva takes three countless aeons to reach the tenth ground and it should be known from other sources how he or she attains the enlightened Form Body by practising the additional path of Highest Yoga Tantra. Khedrup Rinpoche also says the same kind of thing in his *A General Exposition of Tantra.* A person, according to him, can attain the tenth ground of Perfection Vehicle by following exclusively its individual path. Thereafter, he or she must practise Highest Yoga Tantra in order to achieve supreme enlightenment.

Critics say that in both the Perfection Vehicle and the three lower Tantras it is stated that by following their individual paths one can reach enlightenment. This claim according to them contradicts the earlier statements of Gyaltsab Rinpoche and Khedrup Rinpoche. There seems to be a contradiction but there is not. The claims made by the Perfection Vehicle and the three lower Tantras are based on the fact that one reaches enlightenment eventually by the additional path of Highest Yoga Tantra. Were this to happen, critics feel that the Perfection Vehicle and the three lower Tantras cannot be said to lead to enlightenment. It is true that enlightenment is not achieved exclusively by the individual paths of the Perfection Vehicle and the three lower Tantras. Nonetheless, it is feasible to assert that their paths lead to enlightenment.[23] Furthermore, the paths (such as the three principle paths) of other vehicles like the Perfection Vehicle, which were cultivated earlier are not forsaken. Reasoning thus, one can say that enlightenment is achieved by the paths of other vehicles as well.

Critics also argue that as in Highest Yoga Tantra, the three lower Tantras also claim that by their paths practitioners can achieve enlightenment in one lifetime. What then is a special about the same claim made by Highest Yoga Tantra?

Our author accepts the truth of both statements but he explains that the meaning of 'one lifetime' is certainly different in both the classes of Tantra. According to the three lower Tantras a person of sharp faculties, who having completed the yoga without sign, accomplishes a very long life through ritual of longevity and then practices the yoga characterized by non-dual clarity and profundity. Eventually, he or she engages in the practices of Highest Yoga Tantra and achieves enlightenment. But, according to Highest Yoga Tantra the meaning of 'one lifetime' is: even if a person 'newly engages'[24] in the path of Highest Yoga Tantra he or she can attain enlightenment in this very lifetime of degenerate era. By following the path of Highest Yoga Tantra it does not take such a long time for him or her to reach enlightenment as in the three lower Tantras. This in fact is a unique feature of Highest Yoga Tantra.

Part Two:
The Generation Stage

I.B. Specific explanation of the mode of progression on the two stages of Highest [Yoga Tantra].

This has two outlines:

1. The mode of progression on the generation stage.
2. The mode of progression on the completion stage.

The former has five sub-outlines:

   a. Its definition.
   b. Its divisions.
   c. Its etymological explanation.
   d. The criterion of having completed the generation stage.
   e. The mode of transference from the generation stage to the completion stage.

I.B.1.a. The generation stage—Its definition:

> The generation stage is defined as a yoga classified as being a meditation newly contrived or visualized to accord with any of the aspects of death, intermediate state or rebirth. It is also a factor for ripening one's mental continuum by its resultant state, the completion stage, and it does not arise through the [actual] meditational practice of the winds entering, abiding and dissolving into the central psychic channel. Synonyms—generation stage, imputed stage, contrived yoga and yoga of the first stage.

As implicitly stated by its definition, practitioners of the generation stage conceive of themselves as a deity or deities. Their practice is primarily focussed on transforming the three ordinary states of death, the intermediate and rebirth into paths for realizing the three kayas or bodies of an enlightened person. On this stage practitioners are making best use of their imaginative power (mos pa) and skills to practise a deity yoga. This yoga not only accords with the aspects of death, the intermediate state and rebirth but also the aspects of the three resultant bodies of an enlightened person. Briefly speaking, this practice involves meditating on the stages of the dissolution of bodily elements along with the respective deities, eventually culminating in the clear light of death, which is analogous to the Truth body.[25] This is followed by the intermediate state in which practitioners instead of being reborn as beings of such a state they arise themselves in the Complete Enjoyment Body, and then, for rebirth, they arise as an Emanation Body.

When a person dies naturally his or her bodily elements dissolve gradually. The dying person sees certain inner signs and there are observable signs associated with the dissolution of his elements. Initially, he sees a sign like that of the appearance of a mirage as the earth element dissolves into the water element. It sounds as though the physical elements dissolve one into the other but in reality the capacity of a preceding element [to support his body] diminishes and that of the subsequent increases. Consciousness also becomes subtler and subtler during this process of dissolution culminating in the clear light of death.[26]

From its definition it is clear that the yoga of the generation stage does not arise from the winds entering, abiding and dissolving, through actual meditational power, into the central psychic channel. Nevertheless, at this stage practitioners do imagine that the winds enter, abide and dissolve into the central channel. In sharp contrast to this stage, practitioners of the completion stage actually do experience this extraordinary phenomenon. The yoga of the generation stage prepares the mind of practitioners to be ripened by the subsequent yoga of the completion stage. Thus, it is a prerequisite conducive factor for cultivating the yoga of the completion stage.[27] Since the generation stage is a yoga which is classified as a meditation that is contrived to accord with any of the aspects of the three ordinary states of death, the intermediate state and rebirth on the level of the basis, these three are thus taken into paths for spiritual growth. For that reason, as stated in the *Guhyasamaja Prayer (gsang 'dus smon lam)*, we must know the processes of death, the intermediate state and rebirth in order that we can integrate them with the yoga of the generation stage and transform them into conducive factors for our spiritual upliftment. In this connection I would like to present briefly the natural process of death first.

DEATH AND DYING:

The process of death involves eight stages of dissolution of the elements. Initially, our earth element dissolves into the water element; then, the water into the fire element; the fire into the wind element; the wind into the element of consciousness; the consciousness into the mind of white appearance; the mind of white appearance into the mind of radiant red increase; the mind of radiant red increase into the mind of black near-attainment and subsequently the mind of the clear light of death dawns.[28]

These stages of the dissolution of our psycho-physical elements at death are associated with certain external and internal indicative signs. What we mean by one element dissolving into another is: for example, when the capacity of the earth element to support our body diminishes the capacity of our water element becomes predominant. At this point, certain internal and external signs may be observed such as a call out for help as if the body had become heavy and was sinking into the earth. The dying person will have a vision like that of a mirage. This kind of vision usually takes place in a desert where the sunlight strikes very brightly on the sandgrains.[29] From a distance anyone may misapprehend a body of water there. But, this is a case of mistaking a mirage for water.

Similarly, when the capacity of our water element diminishes the capacity of the fire element becomes predominant. The dying person can not talk at this stage and the fluids in his body such as saliva dry up. From the point of view of internal vision there is a smoke like appearance. Subsequently, when the fire element dissolves into the wind element the dying person loses the warmth of his body. If the person is to be reborn in any of the three lower realms it is said that initially the warmth leaves the upper part of his body. On the other hand if he is to be reborn in a higher realm the warmth of his body leaves the feet initially. There is an internal appearance like that of fireflies at this stage.

When the wind dissolves into the element of space/consciousness, the dying person almost ceases to breathe. He might even be declared dead clinically. The sense organs also cease to function. At this stage there is an internal appearance like that of a sputtering butter lamp.

Subsequently, as the consciousness first dissolves into the mind of appearance the dying person sees a radiant white appearance. This internal vision is caused by the falling of the white drop we have received from our father which usually abides at the crown. This appearance is likened to the clear autumn sky pervaded by moonlight. As the mind of the radiant white appearance dissolves into the mind of increase there is an appearance of a radiant redness. This is caused by the ascending of the red drop we have received from our mother; its usual seat is at the navel. This radiant redness is likened to the appearance of the bright red colour of the setting sun.

Later, when the mind of radiant red increase dissolves into the mind of near-attainment there is an appearance of darkness. This internal appearance is induced by a collision of the red and the white drops as they encompass the 'indestructible drop' at the heart. This black appearance is like that of darkness covering the night sky. These three (minds of) appearances have only internal signs of dissolution. Finally, when the mind of black near-attainment dissolves, the subtlest mind of the clear light of death dawns. On this stage, except for the subtlest mind of clear light (which is explained in Buddhist Tantra alone and not even in its Sutra), all other coarse consciousnesses, and even the minds of the three appearances, have already ceased to function. Excepting the appearance of vacuity there is no other appearances for this clear light mind. The red and the white drops[30] we have received from our parents, as mentioned earlier, encompass the 'indestructible drop' (mi gzhig pa'i thig le). It is transparent and is simply called 'indestructible' for it remains as such from the womb to tomb. This drop is 'temporarily indestructible' and it is the seat of the most subtle wind and mind. This subtle wind and mind which is also referred to as 'indestructible drop' remains for ever as indestructible continuing from one life into another. For this reason, it is the 'ultimate indestructible drop'. The period of clear light begins with the cessation of the mind of black near-attainment and it ends with the opening of the seat like 'indestructible drop'.[31] The intermediate state begins with the arisal of the mind of near-attainment as the entire eight stage process of dissolution reverses itself. A qualified lama or a practitioner can abide in the state of clear light by using it as a subjective mind to apprehend emptiness whereby the duration of the clear light of death can be prolonged.[32]

Generally speaking, at death a vacuity appears to our mind of clear light, but that is not emptiness. It is, however, possible for our mind of clear light to see emptiness, provided we have ascertained and developed intimacy with it. Mostly we are not even aware of the dawning of clear light, let alone ascertaining emptiness by it. In order to remain wakeful in the clear light of death and also for it to perceive emptiness we have to study meditational techniques and practise them consistently.

My brief explanation of the process of death and dying is not meant to be a general description of the death of all types of beings; it pertains to the natural death of only womb-born human beings with six constituents of our world.[33] The dissolution process in such a case is gradual and complete. However, for a person who is shot and dies suddenly for instance, his natural process of death is disrupted. As the process of death and dying is fast, so would be the dissolution of elements and coming into existence of the intermediate state. Most likely he will not be able to see through the whole process of dying and experience all the indicative signs mentioned before.

Concerning how long does the process of death and dying last, there is no uniformity as such. In some cases the process lasts for a couple of hours for the dissolution of the elements take that long, and in others it may take even a day or more. Interestingly enough, when the earth element dissolves into the water element a dying person can still talk; we can ask him about the experiences. I recall the death of my class-mate after a prolonged illness. Sitting at the side of my dying friend, he told me that he was seeing all the surroundings as yellow and also felt as if he was sinking into the earth. This yellow vision he had indicated happy rebirth; it is none of the external signs of death. I asked him whether he had finished his daily commitments, to which replied he had finished some short prayers but not the long Sadhana or Liturgical texts of Guhyasamaja, Yamantaka and Vajrayogini. I invited some monks to his death-bed to do those liturgies for him. When they were in the middle of the *Vajrayogini Liturgy* the dying friend breathed his last. The process of his death lasted for more than two hours.

An Intermediate State (Bardo):

As we have seen earlier, the yoga of the generation stage involves cultivating a path on the level of the basis for transforming the three ordinary states: death, the intermediate state and rebirth, into the three resultant bodies of an enlightened person. The intermediate state begins when the mind and body are separated from each other. In general there are four possible ways of taking birth in various states of cyclic existence: from womb, from eggs, from heat and moisture, and by the power of miracles. Of these four ways, all the beings of the intermediate state are born miraculously. It is said that the form of a being of the intermediate state resembles the form of whatever type of rebirth he is going to achieve. The *Treasury of Knowledge (mngon pa mdzod)* says, "The body of a being in the intermediate state is the same as the coming rebirth because they—the two bodies or forms—result from the same karmic action."

There is also mention of the colours of beings in the intermediate state as a pointer of their future rebirths. It is stated that those who will be reborn in hell look like a charred log; those who will be reborn as animals look like smoke; those who will be reborn as hungry ghosts look like water; those who will be reborn as gods (devas) or humans of the desire realm appear yellow and those who will reborn as gods of the form realm appear white. There is no mention of the colour of those who will be reborn as gods of the formless realm as they do not have to pass through the intermediate state. In short, every sentient being in cyclic existence dies to be reborn again.

Also, it is stated that those beings in the intermediate state who will be reborn in hell, walk upside down or on their heads; those who will be reborn as humans or gods of the desire realm walk looking upward or with their heads-in-air and those who will be reborn as hungry ghosts walk backwards.

Acharya Vasubandu described beings in the intermediate state as having miraculous powers for travelling wherever they want to excepting the womb of a mother without obstructions. Karmically they are constrained by the wombs of their mothers. The reason why such beings can not be obstructed even by walls and mountains is due to their subtle unobstructive bodies. They have all the senses intact.

Unlike us humans, hell beings, as well as the gods of the form and of the formless realms have a specified lifespan. Similarly, a being of the intermediate state lives for seven days after which, if it does not find a place for rebirth, it will experience a small death. This process may continue for forty nine days. After forty nine days[34] it will definitely find a place for rebirth—good or bad.

Sometimes eminent lamas and practitioners who pass away do not return soon to our world. We may wonder if they stay throughout the interval period in the intermediate state. But, they don't. They have either been to 'Pure Land' (dag zhing) or other planets to work for beings there. Because of having gained control over their lives they can choose their rebirth. They return to the world heeding our fervent prayer-requests and understanding that they could benefit us further spiritually.

A REBIRTH:

As our body and consciousness part from each other at death so do the subtle body and mind of a being in the intermediate state when he dies. If such a being is going to be reborn as a human, he sees a prospective father and a mother sleeping together. Becoming angry at the sight he dies and his consciousness enters the mother's womb. Having been conceived in the womb he passes through the five stages of foetal development as follows:[35]

1. Oval foetus (mer mer po) which is fluid within but covered by a milk cream like layer from without.
2. Viscous foetus (ltar ltar po) which is solidified from both within and without and is like yogurt but still it has not become flesh.
3. Soft fleshy foetus (gor gor po) which can not resist pressure.
4. Hard fleshy foetus ('khrang 'gyur) which can resist pressure.
5. Development of limbs (rkang lag 'gyus pa)—at this stage the five protrusions of head, the two arms and the two thighs occur.

If the child is to be born as a male he crouches to the right (of the mother's womb) facing his mother's back, whereas a female crouches to the left of the womb facing mother's front. Generally speaking, it takes nine months and ten days for a child to be born. When the time comes for birth, the karmic wind causes the child to be upside down and it takes birth. After the birth life passes through another five stages as follows: childhood, youth, adulthood, middle age, and old age followed by death.

How can we put an end to this cycle of compulsive death, the intermediate state and rebirth? From time immemorial until now we have been wandering in this cyclic existence. We can follow the paths of the Perfection Vehicle and the three lower Tantras to break this cycle, but these will take a long time to do that. However, by the path of Highest Yoga Tantra we can break this cycle very quickly even in this short lifetime. That is because the two stages of the path of Highest Yoga Tantra, and especially the Guhyasamaja Tantra, involve taking the three resultant bodies of a Buddha into the paths which also accord with aspects of death, the intermediate state and rebirth.

GENERATING THE BODY MANDALA AND TAKING THE TRUTH BODY IN THE PATH:

In this connection I shall explain briefly here how to take the three resultant bodies of a Buddha into the paths according to Guhyasamaja Tantra. We must at first generate ourselves into the complete form of the principal deity (Hatred Vajra/Akshobhya) with blue body, three faces, and six arms, etc.[36] And then, set forth the remaining deities of the mandala at various parts of our body. Later, when we dissolve our psycho-physical elements in accordance with the natural process of their dissolution at death, we must simultaneously dissolve the deities associated with them. Even though we may not see the actual signs of the dissolution of the elements and the deities associated with them during our meditational practice, nevertheless, it is important for us to imagine and feel that we are seeing the respective indicative signs.

The way to generate a complete body mandala is as follows: having fully generated ourselves into the principal deity, we then visualize white Vairochana at the crown, red Amitabha at the throat, blue Akshobhya is seen as inseparably one with the principal deity, yellow Ratnasambhava at the navel and green Amoghasiddhi at the groin. All of them arise from the purified factors of our five physical and mental aggregates. Each of them has three faces and six arms.

Subsequently, we visualize the four consorts arising from the puri- fied factors of our four elements at the various parts of our body as follows: green Tara at the crown embracing Vairochana, red Pandaravasini at the throat embracing Amitabha, blue Mamaki at the heart and the white Lochana at the navel embracing Ratnasambhava. Each of them also has three faces and six arms.

And then, we visualize at our two eyes white Kshitigarbhas,[37] at the ears yellow Vajrapanis, at the nose yellow Akashagharba, at the tongue red Lokeshevara, at the heart red Manjushri, at the tip of the Vajra organ green Sarvanirvana-viskambini. If we can, visualize three hun- dred and sixty green Samantabhadras at the three hundred and sixty joints of our body or else just one green Samantabhadra at the chest. Then, visualize white Maitreya on the crown of our head but right in front of Vairochana embracing Tara.

Likewise, visualize at the eyes white Rupavajras embracing

Kshitigarbhas, at the ears yellow Shabdavajras embracing Vajrapanis, at the nose red Gandhavajra embracing Khagharba, at the tongue green Rasavajra embracing Lokeshvara and at the vajra organ blue Sparshavajra embracing Sarvanirvana-viskambini. So far up to this point we have visualized the five Dhyana Buddhas, four consorts, eight Bodhisattvas and five vajra females.

Subsequently, visualize black Yamantakrit at the base of the right thumb, white Aparajita/Prajnantakrit at the base of the left thumb, red Hayagriva at the mouth, blue Vignantakrit at the tip of the vajra organ, black Achala at the joint of the right shoulder, blue Takiraja at the joint of the left shoulder, blue Niladanda at the right knee, black Mahakala at the left knee, blue Ushnishchakravartin behind Vairochana on the crown of our head and black Sumbharajas at the two soles of our feet. All the deities of Guhyasamaja have three faces and six arms.

We must know these deities of the body mandala, their locations in it and the respective constituents of our body they are associated with, in order for us to meditate on the process of death and take it as a path to actualize the Truth Body ('chi wa chos sku lam 'khyer). Our practice here involves dissolving these deities along with our psycho-physical elements. Before dissolving them we should once again reinforce their divine clarity and divine pride.

And then, dissolve them as follows: as the earth element dissolves into the water, the deities associated with the earth element also dissolve. They are: Vairochana at the crown, Lochana at the navel, Kshitigarbhas and Rupavajras at the eyes, Maitreya at the crown, Yamantakrit at the base of the right thumb and Achala at the right shoulder. Having dissolved them, feel that we are seeing an appearance like that of a mirage. At this point we may not see the actual signs of dissolution as at death, however, we imagine seeing them. We also anticipate seeing subsequently the next sign.

Similarly, when the water element dissolves into the fire element all the deities associated with the water dissolve simultaneously. They are: Ratnasambhava at the navel, Mamaki at the heart, Vajrapanis and Shabdavajras at the ears, Aparajita at the base of the left thumb and Takiraja at the left shoulder. When they have dissolved, feel that we are seeing an appearance like that of smoke. Anticipating the next sign, we set forth a strong motivation for it and also reinstate our motivation to meditate well on the all-empty clear light mind when it dawns.

Next, when the fire element dissolves into wind, the deities associated with the fire element also dissolve. They are: Amitabha and Pandaravasini at the throat, Akashagarbha and Gandhavajra at the nose, Hayagriva at the mouth and Niladanda at the right knee. After their dissolution, feel that we are seeing an appearance like that of fire flies and we will subsequently see an appearance like that of a sputtering butter lamp.

Subsequently, when the wind element dissolves into the element of consciousness, the nine deities associated with the wind also dissolve simultaneously. They are: Amoghasiddhi at the groin, Tara at the crown, Lokeshvara and Rasavajra at the tongue, Sarvanirvarana-viskambini and Sparshavajra at the secret organ, Samantabhadras at the joints, Vighnantakrit at the secret organ and Mahabhala at the left knee. After their dissolution feel that we are seeing an appearance like that of a sputtering butter lamp. As before, we should review the visions we have already seen and anticipate the subsequent visions.

Now, when consciousness dissolves into the mind of white appearance Ushnishchakravartin at the crown also dissolves with it simultaneously. As before, here also we should feel that we are seeing a radiant white appearance like that of a clear autumn sky pervaded by moonlight. Subsequently, when the mind of white appearance dissolves into the mind of radiant red increase the Sumbharajas at the soles of our feet also dissolve simultaneously. After their dissolution, feel that we are seeing a radiant red appearance like that of a blazing sunset. And then, when the mind of red increase dissolves into the mind of black near-attainment of the clear light, the Manjushri at the heart dissolves together with it. After their dissolution, feel that we are seeing a black appearance like that of thick darkness at night. As we are about to see the clear light itself, we should strongly motivate ourselves to meditate on it well to actualize the Truth Body when it dawns.

Eventually, as the mind of black near-attainment dissolves into the all-empty clear light mind, we as the principal deity Akshobhya dissolve from above and below into clear light. Feel strongly that this subtlest mind of clear light perceives emptiness nakedly. Remain in this state as long as possible.

In order to be able to do this it is extremely important to know the distinctive aspects of the mind of clear light at that level. It has four unique aspects or features. They are:

1. There is an appearance of vacuity, like that of a clear empty sky of autumn, for the mind of clear light and nothing else apart from that.

2. It ascertains the non-inherent existence of all phenomena.
3. It experiences only great bliss.
4. Identify it (the non-dual subjective and objective clear light) as I, the resultant Truth Body.[38]

In other words, we should identify this subtle mind of clear light as the resultant Truth Body that we will achieve eventually. It is essential that all those four features be present if death is to be taken as a path to actualize the Truth Body. If any of them is missing in our meditation, taking Dharmakaya or the Truth Body into the path would be incomplete.

When our meditation on the process of death and dying culminates in clear light, at that point we should think that it is a blissful entity. Great bliss is the best skillful means in Highest Yoga Tantra. It ascertains the emptiness of inherent existence of all phenomena and for it, there is just that appearance of emptiness. This is to be seen as the resultant Truth Body that we will achieve eventually. Those who have accomplished the meaning clear light of the fourth level of the completion stage perceive emptiness directly and non-conceptually at this point.

In general, notwithstanding whether or not one has an understanding of emptiness, all that appears to the clear light of death is empty appearance like space. Emptiness is as an unobstructive phenomenon as the space. Emptiness is a 'non-affirming negative phenomenon' (med dgag).[39] In other words, it is merely an absence of true or inherent existence without affirming anything in its absence. True or inherent existence is the object of negation (dgag bya). Though there is an all-empty appearance for our subtle mind of the clear light of death that it is not an appearance of emptiness. More over, the clear light does not necessarily ascertain emptiness.

Recite the following mantra when the very subtle mind of clear light dawns with all its aspects or features as explained before: OM SHUNYATA JNANA VAJRA SVABHAVA ATMAKO AHAM (OM: This vajra nature of the wisdom of emptiness is me or I). We should stay in this state of meditation as long as we can. When we do not have a clear meditation, review the whole process of generating ourselves into the principal deity, setting the deities at various parts of our body and dissolving them simultaneously with our psycho-physical elements culminating in the clear light. Then, be in this state as long as we can. We can repeat this meditational process a number of times. Eventually, we will reach a level of realization where, due to the fulfillment of intimacy with this practice, without need to make much effort, this whole process of meditation can work on its own accord. It would be much easier to practise then.

To put everything in nutshell, in order to do this meditation well we must know these three essential principles:

1. Ordinary death as the basis of purification.
2. The mind of clear light as the purifying path.
3. The resultant Truth Body as the purified result.

I think many of us have received the Guhyasamaja empowerment and the explanation of its practice from His Holiness the Dalai Lama at the Theckchen Choeling Temple. His Holiness elucidated most wonderfully how to take the three bodies of a Buddha into the paths. Having received such profound teachings we should not leave his insightful expositions at a mere intellectual level. Instead, we must practise his teaching as much as we can. Even if we have to use in our practice, for instance, the index finger to point at different parts of our body for setting the deities of the body mandala and dissolving them, that does not matter; let us do that. That indicates we are trying our best at least.

Taking the Complete Enjoyment Body in the Path.

With that brief explanation on taking the resultant Truth Body into a path, I shall now explain how we can take the Complete Enjoyment Body into a path. This also has three most important factors as follows:

1. The intermediate state as the basis of purification.
2. An illusory body of path as the purifier.
3. The resultant Complete Enjoyment body as the purified result.

Even though we meditate on the Truth Body for the benefit of all beings, in actuality this Body is imperceptible to ordinary consciousness; only Buddhas can perceive each other's Truth Body. Therefore, in order to help and benefit beings with pure karmic dispositions Buddhas manifest themselves as the Complete Enjoyment Bodies. Like them, while in the state of meditation on the Truth Body, we should altruistically think of arising in the form of the Complete Enjoyment Body. This body arises by way of what is known as the 'five modes of perfect enlightenment' (mngon byang lnga) as follows.

In actual practice, according to the *Guhyasamaja Liturgy*, our original seat is vacant. Initially we should meditate on the sphere of emptiness. Of the five modes of perfect enlightenment, this is called the 'mode of enlightenment through suchness or thatness' (de bzhin nyid las byang chub pa). On that seat, from within emptiness, there appears HUM which transforms into a sun disc; on it OM, which transforms into a moon disc and on that red AH, which transforms into an eight petalled lotus. On the level of basis, the intermediate state begans along with the dawning of the mind of black near-attainment right after the mind of clear light of death in the reverse process. On the path, instead of being born as a being of the intermediate state, we arise as a Complete Enjoyment Body. This is a very subtle body indeed. In fact, even the body of a being in the intermediate state is not like our body of flesh and blood but a very subtle mental body. Hence, it is beyond the range of our senses. It is for the same reason, the Complete Enjoyment Body is also called a 'Wisdom Body'.

The three cushions of sun, moon and lotus which arise from within the sphere of emptiness correspond to the minds of the three appearances—the black near-attainment, the red increase and the white appearance—of the reversal process on the level of basis. The three syllables: OM AH HUM give rise to the three cushions, and on them are stacked OM AH HUM. These two sets of three syllables correspond to the subtle winds of the minds of the three appearances of the reversal process; and the division into two sets of three syllables corresponds to the division of the subtle winds of the minds of the three appearances into two sets: 'casual wind' and 'co-existent wind'. Each of the minds of the three appearances is preceded by its casual wind and has also a wind that co-exists with it.

The three cushions and the syllables merge into each other inseparably and this corresponds to the inseparability of the subtle body and mind of a being in the intermediate state on the level of basis. There arises a full moon disc which radiates rays of light to the whole of the environment and its inhabitants within. These are withdrawn and dissolved into the moon disc itself. This corresponds to the fact that the subtle mind with its subtle wind' is the source of all animate and inanimate phenomena. Reciting the following mantra: OM DHARMADHATU SVABHAVA ATMAKO AHAM one should identify that moon as I, the resultant Complete Enjoyment Body and hold divine pride. That moon has arisen from the subtle wind and mind. This is known as the 'mode of enlightenment through a moon' (dzla wa las byang chub pa).

Upon this full moon, as bubbles bursting out of water, arise white OM, red AH, and blue HUM. These three syllables on the level of basis correspond to the speech of a being in the intermediate state. They radiate rays of light which invite the Dhyana Buddhas (Buddhas of the five families) in the ten directions with their retinues, and they dissolve into the three syllables. This is known as the 'mode of enlightenment through seed syllables' (sa bon las byang chub pa). From these arise a five spoked white vajra; at its hub we should visualize OM AH HUM. This vajra on the level of basis corresponds to the mind of a being in the intermediate state. This is known as the 'mode of enlightenment through hand implement' (phyag mtshan las byang chub pa).

From the complete transformation of this five spoked white vajra, we arise as a white Primordial Protector with three faces. The front is white, the right face is blue and the left red. He is also adorned with jewellery. This is known as the 'mode of enlightenment through a complete body' (sku rzogs pa las byang chub pa).[40] We should feel that this Primordial Protector is my resultant Enjoyment Body and therefore, it is me or I and hold this divine pride. This Complete Enjoyment Body on the level of basis corresponds to the body of a being in the intermediate state. As long as we remain in this state only Arya Bodhisattvas, who have a direct experience into emptiness, can see us and receive direct benefits but not others including even the Bodhisattvas of the path of accumulation and the path of preparation. While in the state of a Complete Enjoyment Body, we should, therefore, altruistically think of arising in the form of an Emanation Body for the benefit of innumerable ordinary beings with pure karmic disposition.

TAKING THE EMANATION BODY IN THE PATH:

Briefly speaking, Tathagatas embrace consorts in their celestial abodes and from their [seminal] drop of the mind of enlightenment arise innumerable Akshobhyas who fill the entire space. This space could mean something deeper also but here we can think of the space inside the roof of the inestimable mansion. Just in a while they all merge into a single Akshobhya. We lift ourselves up in space and vacate our seat for the Akshobhya. Then, we dissolve into him in the manner of a wisdom being dissolving into a commitment being. Subsequently we become the Emanation Body Vajrasattva who experience uncontaminated bliss. This process on the level of basis corresponds to the mode of entry of the consciousness of a being of the intermediate state into the regenerative substances of the parents. This passage appears in its complete form in the *Root Tantra of Guhyasamaja*. According to the *Bright Lamp (sgron gsal)* it has four levels of meaning, from the literal to the ultimate, illustrating the great depth of Guhyasamaja. For example, its general meaning reveals 'altruistic activities of the deities of instantaneous imagination' (lhag mos kyi mdzad pa) of the Guhyasamaja mandala. The ultimate meaning of the passage is that the five physical and mental aggregates of an illusory body are referred to by the term,'Tathagatas'. They are overpowered by the all-empty meaning clear light which is free of all dualistic appearances and arises after the gradual disappearance of the preceding three empties: empty, great empty and very empty. For details and other meanings of the passage you should consult authentic sources such as Khedrup Rinpoche's *An Ocean of Attainments of the Generation Stage (bskyed rim dgnos grub rgya mtsho)*.

We are now a blue Emanation Body Vajrasattva with three faces—the front is blue, the right white and the left red.

The three essential principles of taking an Emanation Body into the path are:

1. Ordinary birth, precipitated by contaminated karmic actions and delusions, is the basis of purification.
2. The generation stage is the purifying path.
3. The Emanation Body is the purified result.

Generating the Body into the Residence Mandala:

Prior to generating the thirty two deities of our body mandala[41] we have to generate our body into residence mandala for them as follows.

Visualize that the front, back and the two sides of our body form the four corners of the walls of the mansion; the mouth, nose, anus and urethra form the four doors; the five coloured wind energies, as the basis of conceptions, form the five fold layers of the walls which are white, yellow, red, green and blue; tongue consciousness becomes the precious moulding; intestines become jewelled nets; the sinews and so forth become half nets; a certain portion of the white drop of the mind of enlightenment becomes the half moons; eye consciousness becomes the mirrors; nose consciousness becomes garlands of flowers; tongue sense becomes the bells; body sense becomes the yak tail fans adorning the jewel nets and half nets; ear and body consciousnesses become the banner and pendants on the parapet; the two shins, thighs, forearms and upper arms become the eight pillars; the belly becomes the interior vases; the ear sense becomes the half-moon adorned with vajras at the four corners; the five pure physical and mental aggregates such as form become the five colours of the mansion—white, yellow, red, green, blue; the secret place, navel, heart and the tip of nose become the four arches; the eye sense becomes the wheel of Dharma and the mental consciousness becomes a buck and a doe on the top depicted over the eastern door; the nose sense becomes the banners on the four arches and the mental sense becomes the lotus in the center of the mansion. In this way the different parts of our body are transformed into the residence mandala.

Territorial Boundaries of the Deities and their Source Syllables:

Earlier, in the context of taking the Truth Body into path, I explained how to set forth deities at various parts of our body. Here I will explain in greater detail the territorial boundary of the deities and also their specific source syllables.

In between the crown and the hair line, from white OM in the nature of our form aggregate[42] comes white Vairochana with three faces—white, black, red—and six arms of which the rights hold a wheel, a vajra and a lotus, and the lefts a jewel, a sword and a bell.

In between the hairline and the throat, from red AH in the nature of the aggregate of discriminative awareness comes red Amitabha with three faces—red, black and white—and six arms of which the upper left holds a bell and a red lotus by its stem; the upper right holds a blooming lotus at the heart and the other right hands hold a vajra and a wheel and the lefts a jewel and a sword.

In between the throat and the heart, from blue HUM in the nature of the aggregate of consciousness arises blue Akshobhya with three faces—blue, white and red—and six arms of which the rights hold a vajra, a wheel and a lotus and the lefts a bell, a jewel and a sword.

In between the heart and the navel, from yellow SVA in the nature of the aggregate of feelings arises yellow Ratnasambhava with three faces yellow, black and white—and six arms of which the rights hold a jewel, a vajra and a wheel and the lefts a bell, a yellow lotus and a sword.

In between the navel and the groin, from green HA in the nature of the aggregate of compositional factors arises green Amoghasiddhi with three faces—green, black and white—and six arms of which the rights hold a sword, a crossed vajra and a wheel and the lefts a bell, green lotus and a jewel. All of the five Dhyana Buddhas are crowned with Akshobhya (Buddha).

NEXT, THE FOUR FEMALE CONSORTS ARISE FROM THE PURE ELEMENTS OF OUR BODY.

At the navel, from yellow LAM in the nature of the body's earth element arise Lochana with three faces—white, black and red—and six arms of which the rights hold a wheel, a vajra and a white lotus and the lefts a bell, a jewel and a sword.

At the heart, from blue MAM in the nature of the body's water element arises blue Mamaki with three faces—blue, white and red—and six arms of which the rights hold a vajra, a wheel and a purple lotus and the lefts a bell, a jewel and a sword.

At the throat, from red PAM in the nature of the body's fire element arises red Pandaravasini with three faces—red, black and whi te—and six arms of which the upper left holds a bell and the stem of a red lotus and the upper right holds a blooming lotus at the heart; the remaining rights hold a vajra and a wheel and the lefts a jewel and a sword.

At the crown, from green TAM in the nature of the body's wind element arises green Tara with three faces—green, black and white— and six arms of which the rights hold a crossed vajra, a wheel and a lotus marked by a vajra and the lefts a bell, a jewel and a sword.

Of the four consorts Lochana is crowned with Vairochana, Mamaki is crowned with Akshobhya, Pardaravasini is crowned with Amitabha and Tara is crowned with Amoghasiddhi. (These Tathagatas are the lords of their families.)

Similarly, from the pure factors of the senses, joints, sinews and the five sensual objects conjoined with the mental continuum arise the eight Bodhisattvas and the female consorts as follows:

At the two eyeballs, from THILMs in the nature of the eye sense faculty arise white Kshitigarbhas crowned by Vairochana, with three faces—white, black, and red—and six arms of which the rights hold a wheel, a vajra and a white lotus and the lefts a bell, a jewel and a sword.

At the doors to the eyes, from DZAs in the nature of the forms conjoined with the mindstream arise white Rupavajras, crowned by Vairochana, with three faces—white, black and red—and six arms of which the two upper hands hold a red mirror and the remaining rights hold a vajra and a white lotus and the lefts a jewel and a sword. They embrace Kshitigarbhas.

At the ears, from OMs in the nature of the ear sense faculty arise yellow Vajrapanis crowned by Ratnasambhava, with three faces—yellow, black, and white—and six arms of which the rights hold a jewel, a vajra and a wheel and the lefts a bell, a yellow lotus, and a sword.

At the doors to the ears, from HUMs in the nature of the sounds conjoined with the mindstream arise yellow Shabdavajras crowned by Ratnasambhava with three faces—yellow, black and white—and six arms of which the upper hands play a blue lute and the remaining rights hold a wheel and a purple lotus and the lefts a jewel and a sword. They embrace Vajrapanis with the first pair of their arms.

At the nose, from OM in the nature of the nose sense faculty arises yellow Akashagharbha crowned by Ratnasambhava with three faces—yellow, black, and white—and six arms of which the rights hold a jewel, a vajra and a wheel and the lefts a bell, a yellow lotus and a sword.

At the door to the nose, from BAM in the nature of smell conjoined with the mindstream arises red Gandhavajra crowned by Amitabha, with three faces—red, black and white—and six arms of which the two upper hands hold a conch shell of scent and the remaining rights hold a vajra and a wheel and the lefts a jewel and a sword. She embraces yellow Akshagharbha.

At the tongue, from OM in nature of the tongue sense faculty arises red Lokeshvara crowned by Amitabha with three faces—red, black and white—and six arms of which the upper left holds a bell and a red lotus by its stem and the upper right holds a blooming lotus at the heart; the remaining rights hold a vajra and a wheel and the lefts a jewel and a sword.

At the door to the mouth, from HOH in the nature of taste conjoined with the mindstream arises green Rasavajra crowned by Amoghasiddhi with three faces—green, black and white—and six arms of which the two upper hands hold a vessel of flavours and the remaining rights hold a wheel and a lily marked by a vajra and the lefts a jewel and a sword. She embraces Lokeshvara.

At the heart, from HUM in the nature of the mental sense faculty arises red Manjushri crowned by Amitabha with three faces—red, black and white—and six arms of which the upper left holds a bell and a red lotus by its stem and the upper right a blooming lotus at the heart; the remaining rights hold a vajra and a wheel and the lefts a jewel and a sword. He has no consort.

At the vajra organ, from OM in the nature of the body sense faculty arises green Sarvanirvarana-viskhambhini crowned by Amoghasiddhi with three faces—green, black and white—and six arms of which the rights hold a sword, a crossed vajra and a wheel and the lefts a bell, a green lotus and a jewel.

At the opening of the vajra organ, from KHAM in the nature of the objects of touch conjoined with the mindstream arises blue Sparshavajra crowned by Akshobhya with three faces—blue, white and red—and six arms of which the rights hold a vajra, a wheel and a lotus and the lefts a bell, a jewel and a sword. She embraces Sarvanirvarana--viskhambhini.

At the joints of the body, from SAM in the nature of the joints arise green Samantabhadras crowned by Amoghasiddhis with three faces—green, black and white—and six arms of which the rights hold a sword, a crossed vajra and a wheel and the lefts a bell, a green lotus and a jewel. If it is inconvenient to visualize Samantabhadras at the three hundred and sixty joints of our body it would suffice to visualize just one Samantabhadra at our chest.

At the crown, from MAIM in the nature of the nerves and the sinews arises white Maitreya crowned by Vairochana with three faces—white, black and red—and six arms of which the rights hold a Naga plant's flower marked by a wheel, a vajra and a white lotus and the lefts a bell, a jewel and a sword.

All the deities from Vairochana to Maitreya are adorned with precious jewellery from the crown to the anklets and also variegated attires of silks.

As for the ten wrathful or fierce protectors, we should visualize them as follows at their seats on our body.

At the base of the right thumb, from HUM in the nature of the right hand arises black Yamantakrit crowned by Vairochana with three faces—black, white and red—and six arms of which the rights hold a staff, a wheel and a vajra and the upper left holds over the chest with threatening gesture a noose and the remaining lefts a bell and an axe.

At the base of the left thumb, from HUM in the nature of the left hand arises white Prajnantakrit crowned by Ratnasambhava with three faces—white, black and red—and six arms of which the rights hold a vajra, a white staff marked by a vajra and a sword and the upper left holds over the chest with threatening gesture a noose and the remaining lefts a bell and an axe.

At the mouth, from HUM in the nature of mouth arises red Hayagriva crowned by Amitabha with three faces—red, black and white—and six arms of which the rights hold a lotus, a sword and a pounder and the lefts a bell on the hip, an axe and a noose.

At the vajra organ, from HUM in the nature of the vajra organ arises black Vighnantakrit crowned by Amoghasiddhi with three faces—blue, white and red—and six arms of which the rights hold a crossed vajra, a wheel and a spear and the upper left holds over the chest with threatening gesture a noose and the remaining lefts a bell and an axe.

At the right shoulder, from HUM in the nature of the right shoulder arises black Achala crowned by Vairochana with three faces—black, white and red—and six arms of which the rights hold a sword, a vajra and a wheel and the upper left holds over the chest a threatening gesture and the remaining lefts an axe and a noose.

At the left shoulder, from HUM in the nature of the left shoulder arises blue Takkiraja crowned by Ratnasambhava with three faces—black, white and red—and six arms of which the first two hands perform the Humkara gesture and the remaining rights hold a vajra and a sword and the lefts a noose and an iron hook.

At the right knee, from HUM in the nature of the right knee arises blue Niladanda crowned by Amitabha with three faces—blue, white and red—and six arms of which the rights hold a vajra marked blue staff, a sword and a wheel and the upper left holds over the chest with threatening gesture a noose and the remaining lefts a lotus and an axe.

At the left knee, from HUM in the nature of the left knee arises blue Mahabala crowned by Amoghasiddhi with three faces—black, white and red—and six arms of which the rights hold a vajra marked black staff, a vajra and a wheel and the upper left holds over the chest with threatening gesture a noose and the remaining lefts a trident and an axe.

At the crown, from HUM in the nature of the crown arises blue Ushnishchakravartin crowned by an Akshobhya with three faces—blue, white and red—and six arms of which the first two hands perform the Ushnishamudra or the gesture of Crown protrusion and the remaining rights hold a vajra and a lotus and the lefts a threatening gesture and a sword.

Finally, at the soles of the feet from HUM in the nature of the soles arise blue Sumbharajas crowned by Akshobhyas with three faces—black, white and red—and six arms of which the right hold a vajra, a wheel and a jewel and the upper left holds over the chest in the threatening gesture a noose and the remaining lefts a lotus and a sword.

All the ten fierce protectors have flaming ginger hair. Generally, each of the four doors of the inestimable mansion are guarded by two of them; similarly underneath the roof and the surface below are guarded by Ushnishchakravartin and Sumbharaja respectively. Alternatively, we can visualize Ushnishchakravartin above the principal deity but slightly to the front facing the opposite direction and Sumbaraja below the principal deity, slightly at his back facing the same direction as the central figure but watching down.

I have described various colours and details of the deities such as their hand symbols/implements and the lords of their families, but beginners may find it very hard to incorporate all such details in their meditation. However, they need not worry so much about every detail at their level. It would suffice to think of the general outlines of the deities at the various parts of the body. Continually meditating on them will generate more and more intimacy with them. Later, when all the details of both the residence and the resident mandalas described above, as found in the *Extensive Sadhana or Liturgy of Guhyasamaja*, have been memorized we can do a complete and better visualization with clarity.

INVITING AND DISSOLVING THE WISDOM BEINGS:

Having set the complete mandalas, we invite Tathagatas of the ten directions and request them to bestow on us the blessings of their three vajras—the vajra body, the vajra speech and the vajra mind. This is also called the 'dissolution of the wisdom beings'(ye shes pa dbab pa) into the commitment beings.

Imagine that on the crown of your head is a full moon disc in the centre of which is white OM emanating five coloured light and a host of Lochanas who fill the whole of space; inviting Vairochanas, they enter into union with them. Approaching the principal couple we request them, and all the Tathagatas in the ten directions, to bless our body as the Vajra Body; consequently they absorb one into another until only one couple remains which melts into white nectar, which then splits into thirty two drops. One of them is bigger than the others. This bigger drop dissolves into Vairochana on the crown of your head, while the remaining drops dissolve into other deities of our body mandala. And now strongly feel that you have achieved the Vajra Body. Identifying yourself with the Vajra Body, generate the divine pride as follows: I am the Vajra Body of all enlightened beings and recite the mantra: OM

SARVA TATHAGATA KAYA VAJRA SVABHAVA ATMAKO AHAM. It is very important to feel that all the deities of your body mandala have been blessed as the Vajra Body.

And then, visualize that on the centre of your tongue is a red AH which transforms in to an eight petalled lotus; upon it there is another red AH emanating five coloured light and a host of Pandaravasinis who summon Amitabhas and enter into union with them. Approaching the principal couple you should request them and also the Tathagatas in the ten directions to bless your speech as the vajra speech. All the couples dissolve one into another until the principal couple becomes red nectar which splits into thirty two drops; one of them is bigger than the rest. The biggest drop dissolves into Amitabha at your throat while the other drops dissolve into other deities. Now, you should hold the pride of your own speech as the Vajra Speech of all enlightened beings and recite the mantra: OM SARVA TATHAGATA VAK VAJRA SVABHAVA ATMAKO AHAM. As before, it is very important to feel that the speech of all the deities of your body mandala have been blessed as the Vajra Speech.

Subsequently, imagine that at your heart is HUM which transforms into a sun disc marked by blue HUM. It emanates five coloured light and a host of Mamakis; inviting a host of Vajra mind Akshobhyas, they enter into union with them. Approaching the principal couple you request them, as well as the Tathagatas in the ten directions, to bless your mind as the Vajra Mind. Consequently, their passion increases and all the couples absorb into one another until only one couple remains which melts into black nectar that splits into thirty two drops. One of them is larger than the others and it dissolves into Akshobhya at your heart while the rest dissolve into other deities of the mandala. Now, you should strongly feel that your own mind is the Vajra Mind of all enlightened beings and recite the mantra: OM SARVA TATHAGATA CITTA VAJRA SVABHAVA ATMAKO AHAM. Here also, as with the blessings of Vajra Body and Vajra Speech, it is very important for you to feel that the minds of all the deities of your body mandala have been blessed as the Vajra Mind.

Finally, you transform yourself into Vajradhara, whose Vajra Body, Vajra Speech and Vajra Mind are inseparable from each other, and recite the mantra: OM SARVA TATHAGATA KAYAVAKCITTA VAJRA SVABHAVA ATMAKO AHAM. You should at this point strongly feel that you are the Vajradhara whose three vajras are inseparable. In this regard also, the clarity of divine appearance and the divine pride are the most important factors.

Many more benefits accrue from visualizing ourselves as a Buddha. Yoga Tantras state that if we visualize our body, speech, and mind as those of a Buddha, and parts of our body as deities the result that we achieve is complete enlightenment. With that I have briefly explained from taking the three bodies of a Buddha into the paths to blessing our body, speech and mind as the three Vajras.

The meditation of those who practise the generation stage is primarily focussed on taking the three ordinary states of death, the intermediate state and rebirth into paths to actualize the three bodies of a Buddha.

The generation stage is also referred to by other terms like 'an imputed stage,' 'a contrived yoga' and 'a yoga of the first stage'. These are all synonyms. As some of these terms implicate, on this stage we imagine or contrive ourselves as a deity or deities and hold their divine pride.

I.B.1.b. *Its divisions:*

From the point of view of its nature, the generation stage is divided into two:

i. *The coarse yoga of single mindfulness.* Synonyms—coarse yoga of the generation stage and the yoga involved in mantra.
ii. *The subtle conceptual yoga.* Synonyms—subtle yoga of the generation stage and the yoga involved within.

> These terms often appear in Tantric commentaries. A yogi who has completed the coarse generation stage is (referred to as) the 'one supremely involved in mantra' (sngags la mchog tu gzhol wa) and a yogi who has completed the subtle generation stage as the 'one supremely involved within' (nang la mchog tu gzhol wa).
>
> The coarse yoga of the generation stage extends up to the 'Supreme Conqueror of the Mandala' (dkyil 'khar rgyal mchog). The subtle yoga of the generation stage is to meditate on the resident and residence mandalas within a subtle drop.

THE COARSE AND THE SUBTLE YOGAS:

From the point of view of its nature, the generation stage can be divided into two: 1) the coarse yoga of single mindfulness and 2) the subtle conceptual yoga.

1. The coarse yoga of the generation stage is so called because compared to the subtle yoga its focal objects, such as the deities of the mandala, are coarse in their aspects. It is deity yoga that involves a single pointed mindfulness of a deity or deities. It is also called a 'yoga supremely involved in mantra' (sngags la mchog tu gzhol va' rnal 'byor); here 'mantra' simply refers to the coarse generation stage.

2. The subtle yoga[43] is so called because compared to the coarse yoga its focal objects, such as the deities, are subtle in their aspects. It is also called a 'yoga supremely involved within' (nang la mchog tu gzhol va' rnal 'byor). For example, within a spot of light on the tip of the nose a practitioner can visualize both the residence and the resident mandalas. Alternatively, a practitioner can visualize a mantra circle—the tiny circle superceding HUM—at the heart and within it a complete residence and resident mandala of Guhyasamaja. Or a practitioner can visualize the complete residence and the resident mandala of Guhyasamaja within a substance drop or seminal drop at the lower end of the central psychic channel.

The coarse generation stage extends up to the 'Supreme Conqueror of the Mandala' (dkyil 'khor rgyal mchog) in the *Sadhana or Liturgy of Guhyasamaja*.

THE SUPREME CONQUEROR OF THE MANDALA:

I have already explained to you how to generate ourselves into the Emanation Body Vajrasattva. As an Emanation Body Vajrasattva, from our heart emerges a consort of the same [Buddha] family. Reciting the mantra: OM SHUNYATA JNANA VAJRA SVABHAVA ATMAKO AHAM, she is dissolved into the sphere of emptiness. And from within emptiness emerges KHAM, which transforms into a vajra marked by KHAM. This syllable now transforms into blue Sparshavajra with three faces and six arms holding implements. From the respective seed syllables we should generate fully characterized deities at various parts of her body. Before entering into union with her both the vajra organ and the lotus organ must be blessed. As a result of being in union the fire of passions increases and melts the deities of our body mandala. A (seminal) drop of the mind of enlightenment is released by the father into her lotus organ and that it transforms into the residence mandala with all its characteristics along with the thirty-two seats of the deities laid inside. Subsequently, another drop is released which splits into thirty two drops that fall on the thirty two seats of the deities. They transform into the seed syllables of the deities; these syllables also transform into their hand implements. Finally, these hand implements also transform into the deities they represent. In this way a complete residence and resident mandala of Guhyasamaja is established in the lotus organ of the consort.

In order to set the deities on their respective seats[44] in the outer residence mandala we withdraw them individually from the lotus organ of the consort through our vajra path, pronounce the respective mantras[45] such as VAJRADHRK for Akshobhya, and emanate them from our heart[46] into the ten directions. These deities perform the general as well as specific enlightened activities such as helping sentient beings to eliminate their predominant delusion like hatred. As Akshobhya returns to our heart we transform into Vajradhara and subsequently into Hatred Vajra. Excepting Akshobhya, all other deities take their seats in the outer mandala as follows: Vairochana in the east; Ratnasambhava in the south; Amitabha in the west; Amoghasiddhi in the north; Lochana in the south east; Mamaki in the south west; Pandaravasini in the north west; Tara in the north east (these four vajra females are within the first level of the mandala); Rupavajra in the south east; Shabdavajra in the south west; Gandhavajra in the north west; Rasavajra in the north east; Maitreya to the right of the eastern door; Kshitigarbha to the left of the eastern door; Vajrapani to the right of the southern door; Khagarbha to the left of the southern door; Lokeshvara to the right of the western door; Manjushri to the left of the western door; Sarvanirvarana-viskambhini to the right of the northern door; Samantabhadra to the left of the northern door; Yamantakrit in the eastern door; Prajnanatakrit in the southern door; Hayagriva in the western door; Vighnantakrit in the northern door; Achala in the south east; Takkiraja in the south west; Niladanda in the north west; Mahabala in the north east; Ushnishachakravartin at the top, slightly to the front of the central deity but facing west and Sumbharaja below facing east but slightly behind the throne of Akshobhya, the central deity.

According to the oral tradition, which ever direction we, as the central deity, are facing that is considered as the east. Whether we generate the residence and the resident mandalas without or within the lotus organ of the consort, it is extremely important for us to identify them as nothing else but ourselves. On the generation stage we do our practice mainly through imaginary visualization, but when we achieve the completion stage we can experience and witness these things actually happening.

After setting the deities in the external residence mandala we withdraw the residence mandala from the lotus organ of the consort and emanate it for the purpose of purifying the external environment and then dissolve it into the external residence mandala.[47] We should also see all the deities on their seats as being the part of the central deity and hold his divine pride. In our meditation we should identify each of the deities from the central figure to the ten fierce protectors as being ourselves [in a divine form]. We can repeat this process from the fierce protectors back to the central deity, see ourselves as the principal deity and hold his divine pride.

If all this is too much, we can at first concentrate on the general outlines of a deity, such as the main face of the principal deity, and then add more details gradually to our meditational structure. This is the way in which we broaden our scope of meditation. Relatively speaking, we will find it easier to visualize the external mandala than the body mandala because deities of the external mandala are equal in size, whereas those of the body mandala vary in their sizes: some are big and others are small. As for the gradual procedure, visualizing the general outlines of deities first and adding more details to them afterwards is common to the generation stage practice of other Highest Yoga Tantras such as Yamantaka and Chakrasamvara.

That was a brief explanation of the 'Supreme Conqueror of the Mandala' (dkyil 'khor rgyal mchog).

Meditation on the subtle yoga, as already explained, involves visualizing a tiny drop of substance (seminal drop) at the lower end of the central psychic channel and generating within it both the resident and residence mandalas. As before, divine clarity and divine pride are the most essential factors to maintain in this meditation also. In the *Guhyasamaja Sadhana* there is no rite for the subtle yoga of the generation stage, but it is to be practised after the coarse yoga of the generation stage. We have to do this meditation until we achieve stability and perfection in it.

As we have seen earlier, the generation stage is a contrived yoga which accords with any of the aspects of death, the intermediate state and rebirth on the level of the basis. However, if we examine whether or not all its yogas fulfill the characteristics of the definition of generation stage, they do not. However, this does not mean such yogas are not the yogas of the generation stage. They are classified as the yogas of generation stage. For instance, the yogas of 'Consorting with the Knowledge-Woman' (rig ma 'du byed pa)[48] and the 'Supreme Conqueror of the Mandala'(dkyil 'khor rgyal mchog) also do not fulfill the characteristics of such a definition, nonetheless, they are classified as yogas of the generation stage. Undoubtedly, all such yogas are deity-yogas. By a careful reading of the definition, its wordings indicate that only the major yogas of the generation stage have to accord with any of the aspects of death, intermediate state and rebirth, but not all of its yogas. Other concomitant yogas are subsumed by the technical words 'classified as [such]' (rigs su gnas pa) of the definition of the generation stage. Lama Tsongkhapa's *Commentary on the Graded Presentation of Guhyasamaja* says that the yoga of 'Supreme Conqueror of the Mandala' and meditation on the 'Wheel of Protection' (srung 'khor) should be taken as preliminary or auxiliary to the major yogas of the generation stage. To meditate on them is to meditate on the generation stage, but they do not accord with any of the aspects of death, the intermediate state and rebirth.

I.B.1.c. Its etymological explanation:

> The coarse yoga of the generation stage is called the coarse yoga of single mindfulness because its objective basis is coarser than the subtle [yoga's] and it is a yoga being mindful of itself along with deities or single pointedly mindful of deities. The subtle yoga of the generation stage is called the subtle conceptual yoga because it is a yoga of meditating on an imputed objective basis which is subtler than the coarse [yoga's]. These yogas of the first stage are called the generation stage because this is the stage at which [one] generates contrived yogas of the three bodies [of an enlightened being] that accord with aspects of death, intermediate state and rebirth [the bases of purification] and meditates upon them.

In contrast to the subtle yoga, the coarse yoga of single mindfulness is aware of the coarse aspects of deities. Single mindfulness does not here mean mindfulness of a single deity but means either identifying oneself completely with a deity or deities or being single pointedly mindful of deities.

The subtle yoga of the generation stage focuses on the subtle aspects of a deity or deities. Just like the coarse yoga, it is also called by various names such as 'the subtle conceptual yoga' and 'the imputed yoga'.

I.B. 1. d. *The criteria of having completed the generation stage:*

> From the point of view of how the levels of the path arise in the mindstream of an individual [practitioner], the generation stage has four levels: i) the Beginner's level, ii) the Slight Dawning of Wisdom, iii) the Slight Control Over Wisdom and iv) the Perfect Control Over Wisdom. Of them, the first, the second and a part of the third (levels) are considered to be occasions of the generation stage whereas the other part of the third and the fourth [levels] are considered to be occasions of the completion stage.

i. *The Beginner's Level (las dang po pa):*

> It extends from the beginning of meditation on the generation stage up to where the coarse residence and resident mandalas appear clearly when visualized in stages but not simultaneously in an instant.

This level begins from an initial meditation on the generation stage and it extends to the point where there occurs a clear vision of the coarse celestial mansion and the deities within, as and when they are visualized in stages. But, they do not appear as clearly as that in an instant when visualized simultaneously.

ii. *The Slight Dawning of Wisdom (ye shes cung dzad babs pa):*

> It extends from the point [where] one has stabilized clarity of the coarse [deities] simultaneously in an instant up to [where] one does not have such a stabilized clarity of the subtle deities of sources.

On this level practitioners have a stabilized clear vision of coarse deities of the mandala in an instantaneous meditation but lack such a clarity with regard to the subtle deities of sources. For instance, they have a stabilized clear vision of the five Dhyana Buddhas but not the two Kshitigarbhas at the eyes as they are subtle because of their locations.

iii. Slight Control Over Wisdom (ye shes la cung dzad dbang thob pa):

> It extends from the point [where] one has stabilized clarity of all the subtle deities instantaneously, as if they were seen face to face, up to [where] one has not reached the level of Perfect Control Over Wisdom. This has factors of both the generation and the completion stages. It is asserted that from this level one achieves stability of the coarse generation stage.

This level begins from the point where practitioners have gained an instantaneous stabilized clear vision of even the subtle deities of the sources such as eye source in their meditation, as if they are all seen face to face. This level extends up until the attainment of the Perfect Control Over Wisdom. A part of this level belongs to the generation stage and the other part to the completion stage. 'Wisdom' here means both the vision and the mind of a practitioner involved in visualization. This level, which is called 'Slight Control over Wisdom', implies an increase of experience. From this level one has gained stability of the coarse generation stage and also some experience of its subtle conceptual yoga. When one has a clear and stabilized vision of the deities in a subtle drop for one sixth of a day (that is four hours), according to this text one has gained control over the subtle conceptual yoga. Unlike the Perfection Vehicle, in the four classes of Tantra there is no mention of a specific method for cultivating calm abiding,[49] because deity-yoga enables a practitioner to achieve the union of calm abiding and special insight. This is in fact a unique feature of Tantra.

iv. Perfect Control Over Wisdom (ye shes la yang dag par dbang thob pa):

> This is an occasion where after having completed the generation stage one has gained the ability [to fulfill] the completion stage.

Practitioners on this level have not only perfected the coarse and the subtle yogas of the generation stage but have also achieved an ability to fulfill the completion stage. This level, therefore, belongs to the completion stage.

THE CRITERIA FOR THE STABILITY IN AND THE COMPLETION OF THE COARSE AND SUBTLE LEVELS OF THE GENERATION STAGE:

While visualizing the residence and resident mandalas in stages, whenever a genuine experience of the spontaneous pride of a deity along with the clear appearance of the mandalas arises precisely in accordance with the size determined by one's motivation, a realization of the generation stage has dawned initially. Accordingly, one who is on this level is taken for a 'person of the generation stage' (bskyed rim pa).

One could lay out separate criteria [as follows] for the accomplishment of stability in and completion of the coarse [yoga] and the subtle [yoga] of the generation stage.

If, while visualizing the coarse residence and resident mandalas, they appear instantaneously and lucidly, with no confusion of their coarse and subtle parts, and can be maintained for one sixth of a day, free of laxity and excitement, one has achieved stability in the coarse generation stage. If the same thing can be done for as long as one wishes, for a month or a year, one has completed the coarse generation stage.

The criteria for the accomplishment of stability in and completion of the subtle generation stage are as follows: If, when the residence and resident mandalas are visualized within a subtle drop to the size of a mustard seed, they appear instantaneously and lucidly with no confusion of their coarse and subtle parts and can be maintained as before [for one sixth of a day, free of laxity and excitement], one has achieved stability in the subtle generation stage. If the same thing can be done for as long as one wishes, as mentioned before, one has completed the subtle generation stage.

THE UNION OF CALM ABIDING AND SPECIAL INSIGHT:

With the completion of the subtle generation stage one attains fully characterized calm abiding (zhi gnas mtshan nyid pa) since one has attained mental and physical pliancy. Special insight (lhag mthong) into emanating and absorbing deities and their hand implements also follows. Due to this an extraordinary union of calm abiding and special insight is attained. For this reason, no where in the four Tantras is there mention of a method for developing calm abiding apart from deity-yoga meditation. This is because a deity-yoga meditation itself accomplishes fully characterized calm abiding.

I.B.1.e. The mode of transference from the generation stage to the completion stage:

Whenever the spontaneous wisdom of great bliss arises in one's mindstream as a result of the winds entering, abiding and dissolving into the central channel by the power of meditation one is transferred from the generation stage to the completion stage.

As and when, by the force of meditation, psychic winds enter, abide and dissolve into the central channel and practitioners experience the spontaneous wisdom of great bliss in their mindstream, they progress from the generation stage to the completion stage.

Part Three
The Completion Stage

I.B. 2. The mode of progression on the completion stage.

This also has five sub-outlines:
   a. Its definition.
   b. Its divisions.
   c. Its etymological explanation.
   d. The mode of transferance from a lower level to a higher level.
   e. The mode of actualizing results.

I.B. 2. a. Its definition:

> The completion stage is a yoga in the mindstream of a trainee which has arisen from the winds entering, abiding and dissolving into the central channel by the power of meditation. Although on the generation stage it is possible for a practitioner with sharp faculties to experience a realization induced by the winds entering, abiding and dissolving into the central channel by relying upon an action seal (consort), from the point of view of its nature such an experience is classified as a realization of the completion stage.

> Synonyms: unimputed stage, genuine yoga and yoga of the second stage.

I.B. 2. b. Its divisions:

> According to the *Compendium of Deeds* (*spyod bsdus*) and a commentary to the sixth chapter of the *Root-Tantra [Guhyasamaja]* completion stage is divided into six levels as . follows:

   i. Isolated Body.

    ii. Isolated Speech.
   iii. Isolated Mind.
   iv. Illusory Body.
    v. Clear Light.
   vi. State of Union.

But the *Five Levels* (*rim lnga*) and the *Graded Presentation* (*rnam gshag rim pa*), [by Acharya Nagabodhi,] mention five levels [of the completion stage], which include the isolated body under the isolated speech, which is explained first. Similarly, the first chapter of the *Bright Lamp* classifies the completion stage into even four levels, such as the level focusing on mind, and includes the first two levels under the isolated mind. The difference between these systems is merely a matter of classification; they do not, therefore, contradict each other.

In the *Subsequent Tantra of Guhyasamaja* (*'dus pa' rgyud phyima*) it is explained that the completion stage has six subsidiary yogas, such as individual withdrawal. Of these six subsidiary yogas, individual withdrawal and concentration are included in the isolated body, vitality and exertion in the isolated speech, retention in the clear light, subsequent mindfulness and meditative stabilization in the state of union.

Practitioners of the completion stage[50] experience the spontaneous great bliss as a result of the winds of their bodies flowing, abiding and dissolving into the central psychic channel by the power of meditation. The completion stage is also referred to by other terms such as 'the genuine yoga', 'unimputed yoga' and 'the yoga of the second stage'. It has six levels: 'isolated body', 'isolated speech', 'isolated mind', 'illusory body', 'clear light' and the 'state of union'. Some texts such as the *Five Levels* present five levels of the completion stage, including 'isolated body' in the level of the 'isolated speech'. Obviously, this is just a matter of classification and therefore, does not contradict with the presentation of the six levels.

I.B. 2. c. *Its etymological explanation:*

The yoga of the second stage is called the completion stage because it is a stage where, without depending on a conceptual imputation, one meditates by penetrating the vital points of the body, such as the channels, winds and drops, that was whole right from its coming into existence.

ISOLATED BODY:

I.B. 2. d. *The mode of transference from a lower level to a higher level:*

The mode of transference from the generation stage to the isolated body of the completion stage was as explained above. The isolated body of the completion stage is a yoga such that while in equipoise one meditates on the wisdom of bliss and emptiness arising from the winds dissolving into the central channel. Waking up from that in the post meditation period, all objects that appear are sealed by bliss and emptiness and arise in the aspect of deities, such as those of the hundred [Buddhas'] families.

The isolated body is so called because it is a yoga that seals the body [the basis of isolation] composed of the aggregates, constituents, sources and so forth within one's mindstream, by the bliss and emptiness of the completion stage. Having isolated the body from ordinary appearance and grasping, it appears in the aspect of pure deities. In general, the isolated body contains parts of both the generation stage and the completion stage.

According to the Perfection Vehicle, the two main obscurations for our spiritual growth are: obscuration to liberation (nyon sgrib) and obscuration to omniscience (shes sgrib). In other words, they are the delusions and their latencies on the mind. But according to the Tantric Vehicle, the two main obstacles for our spiritual growth are: ordinary appearance (tha mal gyi snang wa) and ordinary clinging (tha mal gyi zhen pa). For instance, we perceive our physical and mental aggregates as being ordinary and cling to them accordingly. 'Isolated body' as a yoga isolates them from their ordinary appearance and ordinary clinging. Generating ourselves as a deity or deities of either the family of hundreds (of Buddhas) or the family of five Dhyana Buddhas or the family of the three Lords or the family of Vajradhara, we block[51] ordinary appearance and ordinary clinging and instead see ourselves as being divine and hold their divine pride. As we have seen earlier with the varying classifications of the levels of the completion stage, these 'families of Buddhas' are also just a matter of classification and therefore, there is no contradiction here.

ISOLATED SPEECH:

1.B.2.d. *The mode of transference from a lower level (of the completion stage) to its higher level.*

This has five outlines:

i. The mode of transference from isolated body to isolated speech:

> By relying upon the Vajra Recitation for the manifestation of the winds entering, abiding and emerging to resonate (naturally) with that of the three syllables (OM AH HUM), the channel knots above and below the heart are loosened. Due to this the winds above and below dissolve into the heart channel and consequently the wisdom of appearance arises. When that happens one is transferred from the isolated body to the isolated speech.

Etymological explanation of the isolated speech:

> It is so-called because of its being a yoga that isolates the most subtle wind, the source of speech, from its ordinary flow and combines it inseparably with mantra.

Similarly, ordinary speech or breath, which is the basis of our speech, is isolated from its ordinary appearance and also clinging to it as being just ordinary. Alternatively speaking, the most subtle wind (breath), which is the source of our speech, is isolated from its ordinariness. Imagine that its three-fold activity of inhalation, abidance and exhalation has the natural resonance of the three syllables—OM AH HUM.

I have already explained to you that practitioners on the level of the 'isolated speech' experience the wisdom of appearance. This is due to the untying of the channel knots above and below their heart by the 'vajra recitation', and also the winds entering, abiding and emerging, in the upper and the lower parts of the channel from their heart channel, in accordance with the resonance of the three syllables. This is the second level of the completion stage which is also commonly known as 'vitality and exertion', 'isolated speech' and the 'vajra recitation'. The *Subsequent Tantra* says that it should be called 'vitality and exertion' although 'vajra recitation' and 'isolated speech' are the main yogas.

THE THREE TYPES OF VITALITY AND EXERTION:

Concerning the 'vitality and exertion' level, there are three types: the 'vitality and exertion' of meditating on a mantra circle at the heart, the 'vitality and exertion' of meditating on a seminal drop at the lower end of the central channel or the tip of the secret organ, and the 'vitality and exertion' of meditating on a tiny light circle at the tip of nose. Of them the yogas of meditating on a mantra circle at the heart and a seminal drop at the tip of the secret organ are neither the yoga of 'isolated speech' nor the yoga of 'vajra recitation'.[52] For any yoga to be either of the two ('vajra recitation' and 'isolated speech') it must involve meditation on a tiny light circle at the tip of the nose.[53]

We should allow our breath to flow in and out naturally even when we practise 'vajra recitation'. This practice counteracts seeing the flowing in, abiding and flowing out of our breath as being ordinary and different from the resonance of OM AH HUM. 'Vajra recitation' isolates our breath from this object of negation and we experience the three-fold process of breath resonating the three syllables. This has its source in Lama Tsongkhapa's *Clear Lamp*. He says that 'vajra recitation'[54] means natural resonance of our breath with the three syllables of the three Vajras.

Regarding the yoga of 'vitality and exertion' of meditating on a mantra circle at the heart, practitioners visualize a resplendent HUM at the heart channel. The nada or squiggle of HUM is particularly brilliant; concentrating on it, winds gather and dissolve into the central psychic channel at the heart.[55]

As for the yoga of 'vitality and exertion' of meditating on a seminal drop at the tip of the secret organ, highly realized practitioners can concentrate on such a tiny seminal drop, to the size of a mustard seed, at the meeting point of their secret organs even while uniting with their consorts and retain the drop without being released. This technique facilitates immensely the untying of channel knots at the heart so that the winds can enter the indestructible drop. Others who have not reached such a high level of realization practise it uniting with a wisdom or imagined consort.[56]

As a result of practising 'vajra recitation', with which the three-fold activity of breathing resonate with OM AH HUM, when the channel knots above and below the channel wheel at the heart are untied and the winds dissolve therein inducing the wisdom of appearance, at that point the meditators are transferred from the level of 'isolated body' to the level of 'isolated speech'.

It is called as such for being a yoga that isolates the subtlest wind or breath, the source of speech, from its ordinary appearance and ordinary clinging, combining it inseparably with the mantra. The 'isolated speech' is aware of the innate quality of the natural process of our breath as having the resonance of the three syllables—OM AH HUM. Therefore, it is not a case of simply fabricating and imagining that our breath resonates with the sounds of the three syllables. This is a yoga of 'vajra recitation' which is classified into various types.

Isolated Mind:

ii. *The mode of transference from the isolated speech to the isolated mind:*

> By relying upon an internal condition of the Vajra Recitation of the pervasive wind and an external condition of the Vitality and Exertion of a consort, channel knots at the heart are completely untied. Due to this a part of the pervasive wind along with the primary and secondary winds dissolves into the indestructible drop at the heart, which produces the wisdom of appearance. Whenever that happens one is transferred from the isolated speech to the isolated mind. The *Notes of Khedrup Je's Speech* (*mkhas sgrub rje' gsung dzin bris*) says, "Whichever of the four emptinesses dawns from the initial meditation on the isolated speech up to the point [where] the channel knots at the heart are not completely untied they are the isolated speech. But the four emptinesses of the isolated mind dawn initially from the level where the winds enter, abide and dissolve into the indestructible [drop] within the heart channel as a result of relying upon internal and an external methods which completely untie the channel knots at the heart."

In dependence upon the 'vajra recitation' of pervasive wind as an internal condition and the 'vitality and exertion' of a consort[57] as an external condition, when the channel knot at the heart is completely untied and a part of the pervasive wind along with other primary and the secondary winds dissolve into the 'indestructible drop' at the heart, this induces the wisdom of appearance and one is transferred to the 'isolated mind'. The 'vajra recitation' of pervasive wind means that the pervasive wind has the uncontrived quality of OM AH HUM.

According to Khedrup Rinpoche, no matter which of the four

empties dawn by way of meditating on the three drops before the channel knot at the heart is completely untied, it belongs to 'isolated speech'. But when the channel knot at the heart is untied completely, winds enter, abide and dissolve into the 'indestructible drop' within the heart channel; the four empties which dawn at such time belong to 'isolated mind'.

THE HEART CHANNEL AND ITS INDESTRUCTIBLE DROP:

> In general, the winds may dissolve into any vital point of the central channel, the four emptinesses dawn. Nevertheless, they do not dawn as [clearly] at other points as they do when the winds dissolve at the heart. Until the channel knots at the heart are untied by the Vajra Recitation the winds that dissolve at the heart are dissolved into the heart channel [wheel] but not into the indestructible drop. It is said that when the channel knots at the heart are untied, all other channel knots are also untied. At this juncture [some of] our eminent scholars assert that it is absolutely necessary to rely upon an action seal [an actual consort] to generate the isolated mind. But some critics say, that this reliance is necessary to generate the final isolated mind but not for a mere isolated mind. Still, others say that some extremely sharp practitioners of Highest Yoga Tantra can generate complete paths depending upon an exalted wisdom seal alone. Therefore, it is unnecessary for them to rely on an action seal at any time. As there seem to be diverse views, one should analyze them and find out which of them accords with the thought of Je Tsongkhapa.

Generally speaking, whichever vital point of the central channel is focussed on, the four empties dawn. However, they manifest most clearly if we concentrate on the channel wheel at the heart. Winds also gather into the heart channel. Because the mind and wind, as its mount, are inseparable from each other, where ever the mind is focused, wind also gathers there.

In order to experience the four empties most clearly we should visualize HUM in the center of the channel wheel at our heart. By concentrating on it winds enter, abide and dissolve into the central channel at the heart. While watching the process of the dissolution of our bodily elements, imagine and feel that they dissolve as they would at death on the level of the basis. We should also try to feel as if we are vividly seeing indicative signs of the dissolution process from mirage to the all-empty 'clear light' stage. Especially we should feel strongly that we do experience the four empties sequentially—empty, very empty, great empty and all-empty.

Untill the channel knot at the heart is completely untied, although winds can enter the channel wheel at the heart, they cannot enter the 'indestructible drop'. To completely untie the channel knot at the heart, i.e. to loosen the constriction of the central channel by the right and the left channels, as mentioned earlier, we have to do 'vajra recitation' as follows: visualize a tiny circle of light at the tip of the nose; imagine and feel that the winds which course through the channels resound with the three syllables OM AH HUM. This technique will enable us to untie the knot and withdraw the winds into the 'indestructible drop'.

If the channel knot at the heart can be untied, the knots above and below it will also be untied automatically. These knots constrict the channels, but when the heart knot is loosened the one at the throat (above) and the other below (navel), etc., will be loosened. One should meditate single pointedly and continuously on the mantra circle or syllable HUM within the channel wheel at the heart. When this is done it will facilitate the withdrawing of the winds into the 'indestructible drop'. This substantial drop is called 'indestructible' because it remains as such from the womb to tomb. But that which is 'truly indestructible' are the subtlest wind and the subtlest mind encased within this substantial or seminal drop. Because their continuity exists unto enlightenment.

With regard to the channel knots I have not seen any text wherein it is mentioned that we can see them directly. There is mention of three main psychic channels running through our body. The central channel is described as blue, the right red and the left white. It is stated that normally the winds of hatred and desire run primarily in the right and the left channels. They also constrict the central channel. For this reason it is said that normally winds do not and can not flow in the central channel. By practising Tantric yogas the channel knots are untied; as the winds enter the central channel the two side channels become empty. According to (certain) Tibetan scholars, in order to untie the channel knot at the heart completely, which enables the primary as well as the secondary winds to enter and dissolve into the 'indestructible drop', and realize 'isolated mind', it is a must to rely on an actual female consort. Or else they say that the winds cannot be gathered into the central channel and the indestructible drop. From their point of view a male practitioner requires a female consort to accomplish this and vice versa. It is asserted that there is need to rely on a real consort untill the 'isolated mind' is accomplished and thereafter one could arise as an 'illusory body'. But other scholars say that a practitioner of extremely sharp faculties of Highest Yoga Tantra can generate complete path with a wisdom consort and there is no absolute necessity to depend on an actual consort at any time. The author is telling us, as there are diverse scholarly views on this point, we should find out which view accords with the penetrative insight of Je Tsongkhapa.

Since there is a lot of misunderstanding and misgivings about Tantra, I feel it is of prime importance to know unmistakably at what level practitioners can rely on actual consorts to augment their practice. While in union with actual consorts as the drop of bodhicitta melts and descends from the crown to the throat, practitioners should be able to retain it at the channel wheel there and experience the wisdom of bliss and emptiness. And then, do the same thing at respective channel wheels at the heart, at the navel and finally at the vajra organ and experience the four joys of the sequential process. Subsequently, they should be able to reverse this process and experience the four joys of the reversal process. Those who can do this can rely on real consorts.

The etymological explanation of the isolated mind:

> It is so called because of its being a yoga that isolates the mind [which is the root of everything in cyclic existence and the state beyond] from the indicative conceptions and the winds which serve as their mounts and the mind appears in the entity of indivisible bliss and emptiness.

The 'isolated mind' is so called since the subtlest mind, which is the source of everything that exists in both cyclic existence and the state of liberation, is isolated from the eighty indicative conceptions[58] as well as the winds which serve as their mounts, and then it arises in the entity of non-dual bliss and emptiness.

> Although clear lights dawn at the end of the minds of near-attainment below the [level of] isolated mind they are not explained [separately] in texts like the *Five Levels* and the *Compendium of Deeds*, etc. Taking into account that the clear light is explained in [the context of] the fourth level, they have explained the clear lights of the three isolations sub-

sumed under the [minds of] near attainments. This has been done because an exemplary clear light and its preceding mind of near-attainment are the same in that both are consciousnesses with dualistic appearances and thus can be subsumed into one. Whereas the mind of near-attainment which precedes the meaning clear light is a consciousness with a dualistic appearance, the meaning clear light itself is a consciousness without even the slightest dualistic appearance. Hence, these two can not be subsumed into one. And for the same reason, the meaning clear light is counted as the fourth emptiness.

Although the all-empty clear lights dawn just after the minds of near-attainment of the 'isolated body', the 'isolated speech' and the 'isolated mind', Arya Nagarjuna and Aryadeva have not described them separately like the meaning 'clear light'. Instead they have implicitly described such clear lights along with their respective preceding minds of near-attainment just because they are all same in having dualistic appearances such as the duality of a subject and an object. In striking contrast to them the meaning clear light of the fourth level is inseparably absorbed into its object—emptiness. For this reason the meaning clear light is free of all dualistic appearances—even the white, the red and the black of the three preceding minds of appearances. That is why the meaning clear light is explained separately as the fourth level of the completion stage.

SIMILITUDES OF SIGNS FROM MIRAGE TO CLEAR LIGHT:

The similitudes of the [indicative] signs from mirage to clear light appear on occasions such as the [sexual] union of a man and a woman, falling asleep, fainting, etc., on the level of the basis. On the level of the path, they appear during the conferring of the third empowerment and also at the levels below the Vajra Recitation. However, the actual signs appear at death on the level of the basis and on the level of the path from the isolated mind onwards. Je Tsongkhapa stated this in his *Commentary on the Levels of Perfect Realization* (*mngon pas byang chub pa'i rim pa'i rnam bshad*). Hence, to be precise, the [minds of] appearance, increase and near-attainment as well as the clear lights below the Vajra Recitation also have to be accepted as similitudes. On such occasions, although the most subtle dualistic appearances have not been eliminated, coarse appearances have ceased by the force of the winds dissolving into the central channel. Due to this, various appearances arise from the [radiant] white appearance to the [radiant] appearance of the clear dawn sky. Therefore, on such occasions meditation is done integrating bliss and emptiness. Also, the [minds of radiant] appearance, increase, near-attainment and so forth on the occasions of the path do not arise immediately one after the other. As *Gyaltsab Je's Notes on the Five Levels (rgyal tshab rje' rim lnga' dzin bris)* says, "The wisdom of [radiant] appearance arises through repeated familiarity with [its] causes and conditions explained earlier. And then through repeated familiarity with a collection of their causes the wisdom of [radiant] increase and so forth arise. Hence, these [later wisdoms] do not arise immediately after their preceding [wisdoms]."

Concerning the various indicative signs of the dissolution-process of our psycho-physical elements from mirage to clear light, we can speak of the real signs and their similitudes. Keeping aside the real signs for a while, let us deal with their similitudes first. On the level of basis, on several occasions such as in a sexual union, in fainting and falling asleep we experience the similitudes of signs (from mirage to clear light). And then, on the level of path, practitioners of extremely sharp faculties of Highest Yoga Tantra experience similitudes of signs while in union with actual consorts during the third initiation of wisdom-knowledge. Alternatively speaking, one can experience the similitudes of the signs even before starting meditation on the generation and the completion stages. Also, on the levels of the path below the Vajra recitation, one can experience the similitudes of the signs as a result of the winds entering, abiding and dissolving into the central channel.

Now, with regard to the real signs, we do experience them at death on the level of basis, and on the path from the level of isolated mind onward. Great Lama Tsongkhapa stated this in his *Commentary on the Levels of Perfect Realization (mngon par byang chub pa'i lam gyi rim pa' rnam bshad)*. One of the ways to experience all the real signs (from mirage to clear light) is to rely on a seal or consort as an external condition and Vajra Recitation as an internal condition. Due to these, winds enter, abide and dissolve into the central psychic channel. But, there are other techniques as well.

There are certain indicative signs by which practitioners can know that the winds have entered, abided and dissolved into the central channel. When the winds enter into the central psychic channel practitioners find that their breath goes in and out gently through both nostrils and it does so with equal force. This can be measured either with a finger or by counting. Subsequently, when the winds abide in the central channel breathing through both the nostrils stops. Winds could enter and abide in the central channel, however, if they do not dissolve therein, practitioners would feel uneasiness, as if their bodies were old. As the winds dissolve into the central psychic channel practitioners experience the signs of the dissolution of their psycho-physical elements. These are collectively referred to as the twenty five coarse objects.

In the Tantric literature we come across the word 'killing' in the context of the dissolution of twenty five coarse objects.[59] Do not panic. 'Killing' is an encoded term to implicate stopping of the flow of winds in various channels of our body by withdrawing them into the central channel and the heart channel.

Going back to the indicative signs, the minds of three appearances and clear lights on the path below the level of Vajra Recitation, prior to actual death, are similitudes, not real signs. As for the minds of the three appearances as well as clear lights below the Vajra Recitation, although they do not have coarse appearances (for these have been eliminated due to the dissolution of the winds into the central channel), nonetheless they have not overcome subtle dualistic appearances such as the white radiance. Notwithstanding that, these minds are conceptualized as being non-dual bliss and emptiness sustained by meditation. The mind of all-empty clear light which dawns eventually is like the dawn of a clear autumn sky.

Regarding the wisdoms of white appearance, red increase and black near-attainment on the level of path, they do not arise simultaneously but serially over a period of time as follows: we have to cultivate both the internal and the external favourable conditions for developing each of the wisdoms and generate more and more intimacy with them. This certainly involves a great accumulation of positive energy. On the level of path, these wisdoms have to be generated into the great bliss that ascertains emptiness. And for this, the essential causes have to be cultivated and enhanced further. It is from this perspective the text says that the minds of appearance, increase and near-attainment do not arise simultaneously in one sitting but serially over a period of time.

In that way, after one has attained the isolated mind, then through repeated meditation on internal and an external methods as well as the instantaneous and the gradual dissolution processes, when all the winds such the pervasive winds abiding in the joints are dissolved into the indestructible drop at the heart in accordance with the process [of the dissolution of elements] at death, then the actual [indicative] signs from mirage to clear light arise. Such a clear light is the exemplary clear light of the final isolated mind and it is [also] the final [substantial] basis for accomplishing an illusory body of the third level.

As indicated earlier, practitioners who have already achieved the isolated mind rely on consorts as an external condition and any of the three types of vitality and exertion as an internal condition. Following either of the dual process of dissolution—the instantaneous (ril 'dzin) and the gradual (rjes gzhig)—their winds (such as the pervasive wind abiding in the joints) enter and dissolve into the indestructible drop within the heart channel. According to the gradual process of dissolution, their psycho-physical elements dissolve in the same way as they do at the time of death. They experience the real signs from mirage onward and eventually the exemplary clear light of the final isolated mind. This clear light is sustained by meditational practice, and for the same purpose one could repeat the whole process of meditative dissolution. This clear light is considered as the final basis for accomplishing an illusory body of the third level of the completion stage.

ILLUSORY BODY:

iii. The mode of transference from the isolated mind to the illusory body:

As one begins to wake up from the exemplary clear light of the final isolated mind, which has just been explained, [its] wind is slightly stirred, due to which the mind of near-attainment of the reversal [process] is accomplished. Along with it, like a fish leaping out of water, an illusory body characterized by the noble signs and auspicious signs is literally accomplished as distinctively separate from the coarse body precipitated by ripening [actions]. The wind with five rays of light as the mount of the clear light serves as the substantial cause and the clear light mind itself serves as a cooperative condition.

Thus, to accomplish an illusory body, both the coarse and subtle bodies have to be distinguished from each other by the power of meditation, though they need not be accomplished on different [physical] bases (go sa). As *Khedrup Je's Notes on the Five Levels* (*mkhas grub rje' rim lnga' dzin bris*) says: "An impure illusory body accomplished in this life is distinguished from the coarse body but it is not accomplished on a separate basis (go sa) as it does not have the ability to do so." The *Lamp Illuminating the Five Levels* (*rim lnga gsal sgron*) also says: "As stated earlier, for [an illusory body] to be separated from the old body, it is not absolutely necessary for it to abandon the basis (go sa) of the old body to exist. The same thing can also be understood from the *Bright Lamp* which states that the pure illusory body exists within the vessel of the old aggregates and so forth."

While in the exemplary clear light, by following either of the dual process of dissolution, when one is about to rise from it, as the subtle wind as its mount is slightly stirred, the mind of near-attainment of the reversal process is initiated. Along with it, one arises as an illusory body with all its characteristics, much as a fish leaps out of water. This illusory body is achieved from the exemplary clear light mind and its subtle wind as follows: the five coloured subtle wind serves as the substantial cause and the clear light mind itself serves as the co-operative condition. As an illusory body it is characterized by all the thirty-two noble marks and the eighty auspicious signs. And also, it is distinct from the coarse bodies of practitioners which have been precipitated by their ripening karmic actions. At this level, the illusory body is real as opposed to the previously imagined one.

OUR COARSE AND SUBTLE BODIES:

Generally speaking, embodied beings have a coarse and a subtle body. The former is their visible physical body and the latter is their subtlest wind. There are two ways—the common and the uncommon—by which their coarse and subtle bodies are separated from each other. The common way is the separation at death caused by delusions and contaminated karmic actions. For most people when the psycho-physical elements dissolve at death, various indicative signs from mirage to clear light occur. Finally, the subtle mind and the subtle body of wind separate from the coarse body. This separation is either caused by the precipitating karmic action which had determined our life span or any other karmic action which interrupted our life span; in either case delusions are the underlying causes. The uncommon way is the separation brought about by the power of yogis' meditation. For instance, meditators of a high calibre who practise the transference of consciousness can leave their old bodies and enter young bodies left by others at death. But to be able to do this they require substantial experience. The practice of the transference of consciousness involves a visualization of ejecting one's subtle mind/consciousness from the crown aperture. Alternatively, those who are on the final level of isolated mind can separate their coarse and subtle bodies gathering winds into the indestructible drop within the heart channel wheel with the help of a qualified consort.

With that aside, it is a must for a practitioner to engage in any of the 'three types of conduct' (spyod pa gsum) in order to arise in the form of an illusory body of Vajradhara. As for this, yogis who seek an illusory body for example, work for the realization of the exemplary clear light of the final isolated mind by methods such as Vajra Recitation and the dual processes of concentrated dissolution. Later, as they are about to arise from such a clear light state, the reversal process is initiated and thereby they arise in the form of an illusory body in place of arising as a being of the intermediate state. Subsequently, in place of taking rebirth, they arise as an emanated body and continually engage in practices for attaining the union of the two truths; viz., the union of a pure illusory body and the meaning clear light. This union enables them to achieve Buddhahood in that very lifetime. As a matter of fact, any one who has achieved an impure illusory body will achieve enlightenment in one lifetime.

With regard to ourselves, this sensory body is the coarse body and the subtle body is the subtle wind we have that is omnipresent with our subtle mind. As long as the coarse body functions it predominates the whole of our system and the subtle body does not function. This is especially so for the coarse winds flow in our psychic channels; these winds hinder the flow of the subtle wind and mind. Exceptional case would be to activate the subtle energy through a Highest Yoga Tantric meditational practice stopping the flow of the coarse winds. When yogis withdraw their coarse winds into the 'indestructible drop' at the heart, their coarse bodies remain still and unmoving, and they can see and experience the primordial clear light mind. This mind is generated by them into non-dual bliss and emptiness. From within this clear light state later they arise as an illusory body. This body is achieved as being distinctly different from their coarse physical bodies but it arises on the same basis (go sa) as the coarse body. These two bodies are different, but they are not accomplished on two separate physical bases. Khedrup Rinpoche asserts this in his *Notes on the Five Levels*. He says that a yogi who attains the exemplary clear light of the final isolated mind achieves an illusory body in the subsequent moment. Though the impure illusory body achieved in one life is distinct from the old body, nonetheless it is achieved on the same basis as the old body and at that moment it does not have the power to be separated from the old coarse body since the illusory body has just been achieved.

The *Clear Lamp Illuminating the Five Levels* and the *Bright Lamp* also state that it is not absolutely necessary to abandon the physical basis of the old body in order for an illusory body to exist distinctively from the old body; the pure illusory body exists in the vessel of the old aggregates. According to some critics this statement contradicts another statement of the *Clear Lamp* which says that when the body of the state of union is initially accomplished, it does so on a basis separate from the old body. And it is stated that the pure and the impure illusory bodies are accomplished in the same way.

> Should it be said that such a statement contradicts the *Clear Lamp* which states, "When this body of the union is initially accomplished it is done by way of existing on a basis (go sa) separate from the previous body" and also the mode of accomplishing the pure and impure illusory bodies is explained as being the same. That does not matter because according to the import of the statement an illusory body is initially accomplished in the core of the central channel at the heart, the basis of old body, and afterwards it can exist distinctively outside the old aggregates on a basis separate from the old body.
>
> At the time of accomplishing the pure and impure illusory bodies, one does not arise as a mere body [of a deity] but as a complete residence and resident mandala. As *Khedrup Je's Short Writing* (mkhes sgrub rje' yig chung) says: "On all occasions from the isolated body to the state of union, when one arises as Vajradhara one should do so with complete residence and the resident mandalas." Je Milarepa, a lord of yogis, also said, "One accomplishes deities and their inesti-

mable mansions, etc., from the most subtle, delicate wind and mind."

According to Yangchen Galo, our author, that does not matter. What the statement means is that it is possible for an illusory body to separate itself from the old body and exist externally on a separate basis after its initial arisal in the central channel at the heart (which is the same source basis as the old body). Khedrup Rinpoche states in his *Short Writing* that on all occasions when a practitioner arises as an illusory body—pure or impure, from within or without—he or she does so as the complete resident with the residence mandala but not just a single illusory body. This is an extremely important point to keep in mind, especially when we practise deity-yoga. We do not arise merely as a single deity or a couple of deities but with the complete residence and resident mandalas.

The great yogi Milarepa also says that it is from the most subtle, delicate wind and mind that one accomplishes deities and their inestimable celestial mansion. From this we understand that even the inestimable mansions are achieved from the most subtle wind and mind.

> Such an illusory body is accepted as a form (gdzugs) as it is accomplished from a mere wind as its substantial cause, but it is not a matter (bem po) since its nature is exalted wisdom. The [substantial] basis from which it is accomplished is the primordial body or the mere wind, one of the pair of extremely subtle wind and extremely subtle mind [which share the same nature]. That is, this [subtlest] wind is said to be in the nature of both form and consciousness.
>
> The continuity of this illusory body of the third level is uninterrupted, both in the state of meditative equipoise and the *post* meditational period, from its initial accomplishment until one achieves the meaning clear light. But when the meaning clear light is generated this illusory body is absorbed into the meaning clear light and the illusory body's continuity of a similar type ceases.

The most subtle wind and the primordial clear light mind (as if it were mounted on the wind) are the substantial cause and the co-operative condition respectively of an illusory body. This illusory body is a form but is not material like our body of flesh and bone. (It is a subtle energy-form with shape and colour but not a matter which is a mass collection of particles.) It is a form whose nature is that of the wisdom of great bliss. According to Sutrayana all spiritual paths must necessarily be a consciousness. For this reason, the paths and forms are mutually exclusive. But, contrarily, in Tantra all the paths do not necessarily have to be a consciousness. An impure illusory body is a path according to Tantra but it is not a consciousness; it is a form with the nature of an exalted blissful wisdom. (Because this illusory body has the same nature as its omnipresent concomitant clear light consciousness. In other words, they are of the same entity. With this aside, the illusory body itself is the subtlest energy and therefore, neither a mind nor a mental factor.) Even in Tantra forms and consciousnesses are mutually exclusive. This illusory body of the third level is achieved simultaneously with the arisal of the mind of near-attainment of the reversal process, which is subsequent to the exemplary clear light of the final isolated mind. It exists uninterruptedly up to the point where one achieves the meaning clear light. In other words, an impure illusory body exists as it is from its coming into existence until the meaning clear light is achieved.[60]

When the meaning clear light dawns the impure illusory body is absorbed into it and that 'its continuity of a similar type' (rang gi rigs 'dra phyi ma) is severed. This meaning clear light is the fourth level of the completion stage. It is from this clear light state that one arises as a pure illusory body.

INNER AND OUTER AWAKENINGS OF AN ILLUSORY BODY:

> Eminent Lamas have asserted that if an illusory body is initially accomplished in the core of the central channel wheel at the heart it is called the internal arisal or inner awakening (nang ldang). But, if it is initially accomplished outside the aggregates precipitated by ripening [actions], it is called the external arisal or outer awakening (phyi ldang). However, the texts of the Upper and the Lower Tantric Colleges assert only the external arisal of an illusory body. On the other hand, Khedrup Norsang [Gyatso], Gyalwa Wansapa and others accept only the internal arisal [of an illusory body].
>
> The *Clear Lamp Illuminating the Five Levels* says: "At the time of accomplishing an illusory body from the primordial body of the wind and mind of the isolated mind, it follows the [Yogis'] wish as to whether it arises within or without separately outside the coarse body." Taking this into account

the omniscient Panchen Lobsang Choskyi Gyaltsen Palzangpo asserts both the internal arisal and the external arisal [of an illusory body], stating that according to the intentions of yogis there are cases of [an illusory body] arising in the core of the central channel at the heart or outside. In general, both the modes of arising as an illusory body exist and are, therefore, not contradictory. However, with reference to a single basis [person] they are mutually exclusive. Fearing that it would be too lengthy to give here all the proofs to establish those assertions [I would advise] you to learn them from their respective sources.

Concerning the initial achievement of an illusory body, some eminent lamas say that it arises within the aggregates and others say that it arises without, apart from the aggregates. And some others say both the assertions are feasible. Of these three assertions, the first is called the 'internal arisal,' the second, the 'external arisal' and the third agrees with both. According to the syllabus of the Upper and the Lower Tantric Colleges, an external arisal is a must for the illusory body. But according to Khedrup Norsang Gyatso and Gyalwa Ensapa, an internal arisal is a must for the illusory body. That means it arises in the center of the heart channel.

It is important for us to know the reasons why scholars have these differing views with regard to the 'mode of arisal into an illusory body'. Those who assert an internal arisal do so because an illusory body is a wisdom body; it is unobstructive and hence, it initially arises in the center of the channel wheel at the heart [which is also the source basis as the old body]. But others who assert an external arisal say that it is not feasible that the two bodies can exist on the same basis. However, they say, once the illusory body has arisen externally, it can enter the old body in the manner of an emanation. The third party asserts that an illusory body can arise either internally or externally depending upon the intention of a yogi or practitioner.

Based on what is stated in the *Clear Lamp Illuminating the Five Levels*, Panchen Lobsang Chosgyan says that it depends on the intention of yogis whether they want to arise as an illusory body internally or externally. In general these two modes of arisal are not contradictory. But, they are mutually exclusive with regard to a single practitioner. What this means is that initially a practitioner can arise as an illusory body following either way but not both.

It is difficult for someone like me to comment on the differing views of the scholars just mentioned. They are all authoritative statements. However, I personally find it convenient to assert that an illusory body initially arises within one's own body. This is because when the minds of the three appearances—the white, the red and the black—have ceased, the all-empty clear light mind manifests in the central channel at the heart. Just before the reversal process begins the wind of the subtle clear light is slightly stirred and simultaneously one arises as an unobstructive illusory body. And this is still within the body, isn't it? If we subscribe to the view of external arisal there is a little inconvenience. What I mean to say is that after the experience of the minds of the three appearances and the clear light and before the arisal of the mind of near-attainment of the reversal process, one should find time to come out of the old body in order to arise as an illusory body externally. I wonder if there is any time to do that. What do you think? Moreover, the arisal of an illusory body corresponds to the arisal of the body of a being in the intermediate state. At death, the clear light dawns only after the cessation of all the coarse conceptions of the dying person. Together with the slight stirring of the subtle wind of the clear light, the intermediate state comes into existence. Because the body of a being in the intermediate state is unobstructive, I feel that it arises from within the old body of the dead person spontaneously. Anyway, we should investigate the topic further.

As for the internal arisal of an illusory body, which is unobstructive like that of the body of a being in the intermediate state, it initially arises in the center of the heart channel. Afterwards, it can leave the old body in a visible manifestation to perform beneficial deeds, likened to those of a Complete Enjoyment Body, for sentient beings with exceptionally pure perception. And then, it returns to the old body and perform the activities of an Emanation Body to benefit more beings with a pure karmic connection. The general and the specific altruistic deeds are similar to those described with regard to the 'Supreme Conqueror of the Mandala' (dkyil 'khor rgyal mchog).

From the nominal point of view, the most subtle wind and mind can be spoken of as being different, but in terms of their nature they are inseparably one. The subtle wind has a nature of mind but it is not mind. Similarly, pure and impure illusory bodies have the nature of a mind but they are not mind. They are, in aspects, very similar to an Enjoyment Body. The attainment of a pure illusory body must necessarily be preceded by the attainment of an impure illusory body. The pure illusory body is achieved only after the impure illusory body has been purified by the meaning clear light. It is at that point that the impure illusory body ceases to exist and the pure illusory body arises. Eventually the pure illusory body becomes the Complete Enjoyment Body. A being of the intermediate state for instance, has all the sensory faculties and a form, nonetheless, he is invisible to us for his body is subtle. Similarly, an illusory body is also invisible to us because it is a subtle body accomplished from the reflective potency of an exalted wisdom (yi shes kyi rang snang las grub pa).

Various views of the arisal of an illusory body have been given but out of fear of being verbose the author has not elaborated on proofs to establish those views. For details, the author advises us to consult their specific sources.

ILLUSORY BODY AT DAWN:

> With regard to the time for accomplishing [an illusory body], Je Rinpoche [Lama Tsongkhapa], in accordance with the assertions of earlier scholars, states in his works such as the *Great Exposition of the Stages of Secret Mantra* (sngag rim chen mo), *Thorough Illumination of the Meaning of the Principles of Empowerment* (dbang don de nyid rab gsal) and *Commentary to the Graded Presentation [of Guhyasamaja]* (rnam gzhag rim pa' rnam bshad) that an illusory body is accomplished [right] after the [mind of the radiant white] appearance of the reversal process. But in our system, according to the [relevant] context of the *Clear Lamp Illuminating the Five Levels*, an illusory body must be accomplished simultaneously with the cessation of the clear light on the level of the path, just as the intermediate state (bardo) is accomplished simultaneously with the cessation of the clear light of death on the level of the basis. Therefore, an illusory body is accomplished simultaneously with the [mind of] near-attainment of the reversal process.

Regarding the time at which an illusory body arises, Lama Tsongkhapa quotes other scholars' assertions on this point in works such as the *Great Exposition of the Stages of Secret Mantra* (snags rim chen mo). They are of the view that an illusory body occurs after the arisal of the minds of black near-attainment, the red increase and the white appearance of the reversal process which follows the cessation of the clear light. But our author disagrees with their view. According to him, Lama Tsongkhapa's real view is as stated in the *Clear Lamp Illuminating the Five Levels*. On the level of the basis when the clear light of death ceases, together with the cessation of the clear light the intermediate state beings. Similarly, on the level of the path when a practitioner dissolves the winds into the indestructible drop, exactly in accordance with how they dissolve at death, the all-empty clear light dawns. Simultaneous with its cessation the mind of near-attainment of the reversal process and the illusory body arise. Lama Tsongkhapa asserts that the cessation of clear light, the arisal of the mind of near-attainment of the reversal process and the achievement of an illusory body are all simultaneous.

Twelve Examples Illustrating Illusory Body:

The etymological explanation of an illusory body:

> It is so called because of its being a divine form or body, arising solely from the subtle wind and mind. This can be illustrated by twelve examples, such as an illusion. Since it is not pure of the obstructions to liberation, it is the impure illusory body and is also called a 'Contaminated Wisdom Body'.
>
> Even to have a mere understanding of a mode of accomplishing an illusory body is said to be of immense benefit. The *Compendium of the Wisdom Vajra* (*ye shes rdo rje kun las btus pa*) says: "Just by having a special interest in the meditative stabilization of great bliss, one will come to abide on the beginners' ground and will engage in the [path] irreversibly." Thus, to have a special interest in an illusory body after having gained an understanding of it, is similar to completing the generation stage, the beginners' ground, and one will derive benefits such as those of the one engaging in the path [of the generation stage] as if affirmed in that lineage. This meditative stabilization of great bliss is said to be an epithet of an illusory body.

Etymologically speaking, an illusory body is so called because of being a divine form arisen from the subtle wind and mind which can be illustrated by twelve analogies. The twelve analogies are: like an illusion, like the reflection of a moon, like a shadow, like a mirage, like a dream body, like an echo, like a Gandhara (Spirits) town, like a hallucination, like the colours of a rain bow, like a lightening amidst clouds, like bubbles bursting from water and like the reflection of an image in a mirror.

1. Just as an illusory person created by a magician from a magical substance and an incantation of mantra appears as a real person, an illusory body of Vajradhara with complete characteristics arising from the most subtle wind and mind also appears as a real deity.

2. Just as the reflection of the moon in a body of clean water, the pure and impure illusory bodies also appear to those who have a suitable disposition to see them [like the clarity and stillness of open water].

3. Just as the shadow of a body has the shape of a body but lacks flesh and bone, similarly an illusory body has a complete form but no flesh or bone because of its being a wisdom body.

4. Just as mirage appears and disappears instantaneously, when its necessary conditions are gathered, an illusory body can also appear and disappear instantly.

5. Just as a dream body, an illusory body can leave the coarse body of a yogi, go elsewhere to perform various activities, and return to the old body afterwards.

6. Just like an echo made by shouting into an empty cave, an illusory body exists distinctively from the old body, which arose from previous ripening actions, although the two bodies belong to the same mental continuum.

7. Just as a town of Gandharvas (spirits who are called smell eaters) come into existence miraculously wherever they are born by the power of their karmic actions, similarly the residence and the resident mandalas of an illusory body are accomplished miraculously.

8. Just as in a hallucination; e.g. the moon appearing as two moons to a defective sensory perception, so an illusory body can also appear as a multitude of deities.

9. Just like a rainbow, an illusory body has many colours.

10. Just as lightening occurs from amidst the clouds, an illusory body also occurs from within the old body, and is precipitated

by ripening karmic action. (This goes well with the view of the internal arisal of an illusory body. Even if we think of the external arisal, an illusory body initially arises externally but returns to the old body afterwards.)

11. Just like bubbles bursting from water, the impure and the pure illusory bodies arise from the stirring of the subtle winds of the exemplary clear light of the final isolated mind and the meaning clear light of the fourth level.

12. Just like an image in a mirror, an illusory body has complete form.

These are mentioned in the *Compendium of Wisdom Vajra* (*ye shes rdo rje kun las btus pa*) in the context of a trainee on the path. Of these analogies, a dream body is said to be the best analogy. This is because other analogies simply indicate some features of an illusory body but they can not be taken into path. But a dream body is more than an analogy. A yogi who is bent upon practising 'sleep yoga' can take the dream body into path and generate it in the form of an illusory body.

The analogy of a dream body correlating to an illusory body can be explained on three levels. Just as on the initial level a dreamer experiences four empties before an actual dream, so does a yogi before arising into an illusory body. On the intermediate level, the dream body itself is likened to an illusory body. Finally, just as the dream body can leave the old body, go elsewhere and then return to the old body, similarly an illusory body can leave the old body and then return to it after performing altruistic activities. It is from this point of view a dream body is considered as the best analogy. Alternatively, an illusory body too, like a dream body, arises from the subtle wind and mind.

IMPURE AND PURE ILLUSORY BODIES:

As stated earlier, there are two types of illusory body: the impure and the pure illusory bodies. The distinction is made between the two from the point of view of whether or not they are contaminated by delusive obscurations. And, for the same reason an impure illusory body is also called a 'contaminated wisdom body'. It is stated that to have a mere understanding of how to accomplish an illusory body is of an immense benefit. To this end, the *Compendium of Wisdom Vajra* says that those who have generated an intense aspiration to achieve the meditative stabilization of the great bliss will engage in their path irreversibly. They are similar to the practitioners of the Perfection

Vehicle who have the definite lineage in following a path irreversibly, i.e. not switching over to any other another path. The 'meditative stabilization of the great bliss' mentioned in the *Compendium of Wisdom Vajra* is an epithet for an illusory body. Based on statements such as this, we should develop an intense aspiration for an illusory body. Knowing well the essential external and the internal techniques to penetrate the vital points of our bodies, combining the ultimate view of selflessness with the great bliss and the way to accomplish an illusory body from the primordial subtlest wind and mind, the very basis of the Vajra body, we experience an unshakable confidence in the path leading to an illusory body. Our aspiration for an illusory body is also stabilized. Let alone following the actual path, even the knowledge of such a path developed from listening to teaching will deposit rich imprints on our mind for eventually achieving a rainbow like illusory body. Therefore, we should feel extremely fortunate to able to study texts such as this. However, I must caution you that what has just been said must not be taken to mean that a mere listening to a teaching on an illusory body or a mere understanding of it is enough, as if we do not have to practise the teaching. Practice is a must and the foremost necessity.

The Meaning Clear Light:

iv. The mode of transference from the illusory body to the meaning clear light:

> An impure illusory body engages in any of the three types of conduct (spyod pa) for [periods] such as six months. Consequently, when the signs appear indicating quick attainment of the meaning clear, the yogi enters into union with a seal [consort] and meditates repeatedly on the two types of concentrated dissolution process. Consequently, the [minds] of appearance, increase, near-attainment and clear light dawn. At the time when the spontaneous blissful clear light ascertains emptiness directly, the meaning clear light of the fourth level is actualized. At the time there is the cessation of the impure illusory body, attainment of the uninterrupted path of seeing as a direct antidote to the obstructions to liberation, attainment of the first ground of Highest [Yoga Tantra], and becoming an Arya or a Superior. Moreover, this meaning clear light of the fourth level is attained at dawn when the sky is free of its three faults—sunlight, moonlight and dark-

ness. From this point of view, it is considered as an external perfect realization (phyi' mngon byang). And also, from the point of view of its being actualized at the time when the mind within has transcended its three faults of the white, red and black [appearances], it is considered as an internal perfect realization (nang gi mngon byang). Therefore, if anything is the meaning of clear light of the fourth level it must necessarily be both external and internal perfect realizations. In [this context] the *Clear Lamp Illuminating the Five levels* says: "During the exemplary clear light, there is an objective appearance like that of the clear sky but there is no such appearance for the meaning clear light since for it even the subtlest dualistic appearance has disappeared and [therefore] space [itself, not its appearance] is taken as an example to illustrate its being free of the stains of fabrication."

Those who have achieved the impure illusory body have already transcended the generation stage and the final level of the isolated mind. They engage in any of the three types of conduct for half a month, a month or six months. The time for their engaging in such conduct is when they see certain signs indicating that they are very near to attaining the meaning clear light. Then, they enter into union with real consorts, knowing well and being fully aware of the ultimate nature of sensual objects, especially the contact. While in union they practise either the instantaneous or the gradual process of the dissolution of their psycho-physical elements which culminates in the dawning of the clear light. As soon as this spontaneous blissful clear light ascertains objective emptiness directly, i.e., nakedly without dualism, it becomes the meaning clear light of the fourth level of the completion stage. At that time the impure illusory body ceases to exist and the practitioner attains the first spiritual ground of Highest Yoga Tantra. The practitioner is transferred from the level of the illusory body to the level of the meaning clear light. The minds of appearance, increase and the near-attainment and a clear light could dawn prior to this level but they all perceive emptiness conceptually or in other words through its generic image but not nakedly as the meaning clear light.

Earlier I have mentioned about the 'three types of conduct' (spyod pa gsum). Yogis or practitioners engage in these conducts on different occasions. They do so very skillfully. It may do well to remind you that here we are talking about yogis who have already achieved the impure illusory body but not the meaning clear light of the fourth level. During this interval, in order to augment their practice for accomplishing the meaning clear light, they engage in any of the three types of conduct: the 'conduct with elaboration', the 'conduct without elaboration' and the 'conduct completely free of elaboration'. We shall study these conducts in a while.

ENLIGHTENMENT IN THIS, INTERMEDIATE STATE AND OTHER LIVES:

If a person is able to realize the meaning clear light of the fourth level of the completion stage, he or she will undoubtedly achieve supreme enlightenment in that very lifetime. But there are others who achieve supreme enlightenment in the intermediate state by their Tantric practice. They have already accomplished the generation stage and have also reached the level of isolated mind of the completion stage. Setting forth strong motivation to actualize the meaning clear light of the fourth level, which directly ascertains the ultimate truth, at death they dissolve their psycho-physical elements into the clear light of death and from it arise in the form of an illusory body rather than a being of the intermediate state. On the basis of such an illusory body they achieve supreme enlightenment. There are still others who do not achieve enlightenment at this stage but after seven or sometimes even sixteen lives provided that their vows and commitments are kept pure through various procedural methods such as self-initiation. This is a case of someone who keeps the vows and pledges very purely after having received an appropriate initiation. Even though he or she may not have intensively practised the generation and the completion stages but meets with qualified spiritual guides in successive lives and receive the same initiation again and again from them.

According to the Perfection Vehicle there are two types of result corresponding to the past causes (rgyu mthun gyi 'bras bu): a result that corresponds to a past habituated action (byed pa rgyu mthun) and a result that corresponds to a past experience [of the victim] (myong wa rgyu mthun). For instance, those who have saved many lives in their past lives are most likely to be inclined to do so in the present life also from a very young age; similarly, those who take empowerments and keep their vows and pledges purely in this life will have a natural inclination to do the same in successive rebirths. As for the result that corresponds to a past experience of those whose lives were saved, the life savers will experience long and healthy lives.

Concerning details of the 'three types of conduct' according to *Guhyasamaja Tantra*, you can refer to authentic works such as the *Clear Lamp Illuminating the Five Levels* of the completion stage.

One who has achieved an impure illusory body engages in any of the three types of conduct, mentioned earlier, when they see signs indicating quick attainment of the meaning clear light. Being in union with a consort or consorts they follow either the instantaneous or the gradual dissolution process of elements. This facilitates the dawning of the minds of three appearances and the spontaneous clear light of bliss; when it cognises the objective emptiness nakedly without dualism it is transformed into the meaning clear light of the fourth level. The minds of white appearance, red increase and black near-attainment and a clear light could dawn prior to this level, but even this clear light perceives emptiness via its generic image, but not nakedly.

EXEMPLARY CLEAR LIGHT AND THE MEANING CLEAR LIGHT:

Although the exemplary clear light of the final isolated mind and the meaning clear light are both subtle clear lights and they dawn in a similar way, they differ, however, in terms of the presence of a generic image. The former perceives emptiness through the medium of its generic image (i.e. dualistically) whereas the latter perceives emptiness directly. It may seem to us that one is gross and the other subtle, but both of them, in fact, are very subtle and arise after all the coarse conceptions have ceased to exist. This is somewhat analogous to the difference between the 'level of the Supramundane Qualities' of the path of preparation and the path of seeing with regard to emptiness in the Perfection Vehicle.[61] The former, being a conceptual mind, perceives emptiness through its generic image whereas the latter perceives emptiness directly, as the generic image has been removed. In fact, the path of preparation itself becomes the path of seeing as soon as the generic image is removed. I am wondering whether the exemplary clear light mind, which is a conceptual mind, also becomes the meaning clear light after the dualism is eliminated. Probably it does. However, the text does not make direct comment on this point.

The time when a practitioner achieves the meaning clear light is at dawn. Whenever a person achieves the meaning clear light, he or she is no longer an ordinary being but an Arya or Superior or Transcendental person. Because it is actualized at dawn when the sky is free of its three polluting factors—moonlight, sunlight and thick darkness—the meaning clear light is known as the 'external perfect realization' (phyi'i mngon byang). It is also known as the 'internal perfect realization' (nang gi mngon byang) since it is actualized after all the coarse conceptions—even the minds of three appearances—have dissolved, as they do at death and dying. If anything is the meaning clear light it must be both the internal and the external realizations and it must be attained at dawn. As stated in the *Clear Lamp Illuminating the Five Levels* the exemplary clear light of the isolated mind has an objective appearance like that of a clear space but the meaning clear light does not have even the subtlest dualistic appearance and from this view point it is like the empty space itself.

TYPES OF CLEAR LIGHT:

> Generally speaking, from its etymological point of view, clear light is classified into two: the objective clear light and the subjective clear light. The former is a synonym of emptiness. As for the latter, a clear light which ascertains emptiness by way of its conceptual image is an exemplary clear light and a clear light which ascertains emptiness directly is called a meaning clear light. There are numerous exemplary clear lights, such as the exemplary clear lights of the three isolations and the illusory body of the third level. But for the meaning clear light, there are [just four]: a meaning clear light as a direct antidote to the obstructions to liberation; a meaning clear light which has already eliminated the obstructions to liberation; a meaning clear light as a direct antidote to the obstructions to [omniscient] knowledge; and a meaning clear light which has already eliminated the obstructions to knowledge. All such exemplary and meaning clear lights are also called 'wisdoms of non-dual bliss and emptiness'. However, at the time of the spontaneous exemplary [clear light], emptiness is ascertained through its conceptual image due to which the subtlest dualistic appearance has not been eliminated. Therefore, it is simply imagined that bliss and emptiness have become of one taste. [Contrary to this] the spontaneous meaning [clear light] ascertains emptiness directly; therefore, even the subtlest dualistic appearance has disappeared and bliss and emptiness have [actually] become thoroughly of one taste.

From the etymological point of view, clear light can be divided into two: the objective clear light, which is synonymous with emptiness, and the subjective clear light, which is the wisdom that ascertains objective emptiness. The subjective clear light is of two types: that which ascertains emptiness through its generic image, viz., the exemplary clear light, and that which ascertains emptiness directly, viz., the meaning clear light. Of these, the exemplary clear lights of the three isolations and the impure illusory body are instances of the former, whereas the instances of the latter are: the meaning clear light of the uninterrupted path, the direct antidote to delusions obstructing liberation; the meaning clear light of the liberated path which has already abandoned such delusions; the meaning clear light which is the direct antidote to obstructions to omniscience and the meaning clear light of the liberated path which has already abandoned such obstructions. In the Perfection Vehicle the difference between an uninterrupted path (bar chad med lam) and a liberated path (rnam grol lam) is illustrated as follows: the former is like simply shutting the door after a thief has been driven out, in which case the thief can return at any other time, and the latter is like bolting the door from inside after a thief has been driven out, in which case the thief can not return and enter the house. Both the exemplary and the meaning clear lights are referred to as the wisdoms of non-dual bliss and emptiness but that does not mean they are exactly the same. The exemplary clear light ascertains emptiness through the media of a generic image and therefore it is still a dualistic mind. It is not a yoga of meditative stabilization which combines naturally bliss and emptiness as non-dual but it simply imagine them to be so. In sharp contrast to this, the meaning clear light combines bliss and emptiness within itself into a single taste of reality.

Practitioners of the generation stage before attaining the meaning clear light imagine their clear light as a single taste of bliss and emptiness after dissolving their psycho-physical elements into one another. Later, when they attain the meaning clear light, bliss and emptiness become of a single taste.[62]

THE LEVEL FROM WHICH A BODHISATTVA OF THE TENTH GROUND ENTERS THE HIGHEST YOGA TANTRA:

The meaning clear light is so called for the reason that it is a wisdom for which all conventional fabrications have disappeared due to the subjective spontaneous bliss ascertaining directly the objective clear light of the ultimate truth.

If asked on which [level of the Highest Yoga] Tantric path do Bodhisattvas enter after having reached the final life of the tenth ground by the paths of the Perfection Vehicle and the lower Tantras. They do not enter it from the generation stage and the levels below the illusory body of the third level because the accumulation of merit for three great countless aeons by other paths [i.e. the Perfection Vehicle and the three lower Tantras,] are equivalent to the levels below the illusory body of the third level. Hence, they enter the [Highest Yoga Tantric path] from the level of the meaning clear light. This is so because when, in their final lives [of the tenth ground], they are absorbed into an unshakable meditative stabilization Buddhas of the ten directions wake them from it by the sound of snapping their fingers and telling them: "By that meditative stabilization alone you can not become enlightened beings and you must enter the path of Highest Yoga Tantra." Summoning Devaputri Tilottama (Skt: Tila-uktama; Tib: lha'i bu mo thig le mchog ma) the third empowerment of seminal substance is conferred upon them at midnight whereby the meaning clear light is exemplified preceded by [the minds of] appearance, increase and near-attainment. Waking up from that clear light as Bodhisattvas of the Perfection Vehicle, at dawn they are given the fourth empowerment of words through instructions on the clear light and the state of union. Consequently, at that very dawn the meaning clear light is actualized from which they arise in the body of the state of union of trainees. Subsequently, at the latter phase of the dawn, when the first light of day is about to shine, and in dependence upon the state of union of trainees, they actualize the state of union of a non-trainee. As the *Clear Lamp Illuminating the Five Levels* says, "At mid-night a lama [Vajra teacher] confers the actual substantial empowerment [the third empowerment] relying on an action seal [an actual consort] whereby the [meaning] clear light is exemplified. Then, at dawn one is instructed on how to meditate on the clear light and subsequently to accomplish the states of union. Consequently, the meaning clear light is realized and thereafter, the states of union are accomplished."

It is stated that practitioners of the Perfection Vehicle and the three lower Tantras must eventually enter the path of Highest Yoga Tantra; otherwise their paths alone cannot take them to supreme enlightenment. In this context, a question is raised: from what level do practitioners enter the path of Highest Yoga Tantra if they have reached the tenth ground by the paths of the Perfection Vehicle and the three lower Tantras? They do not have to enter it from the generation stage and the levels of the three isolations because the merits that they have already accumulated over three countless aeons are equivalent to the level of the illusory body of the third level. They have also abandoned the obstructions to liberation. They enter the path of Highest Yoga Tantra from the level of the meaning clear light. Although they feel that being in the meditative equipoise of the tenth ground of the Perfection Vehicle, which is immutable, they can attain supreme enlightenment by that path alone, in reality they cannot. They are overconfident about themselves. At this time the Buddhas of the ten directions exhort them to rise up from the equipoise and practise further, telling them that such a meditative state alone will not bring them enlightenment. The Buddhas summon Devi Tilottama for them at mid-night and confer upon them the wisdom-knowledge empowerment. Being in union with her the Bodhisattva experiences the minds of three appearances followed by the clear light. This symbolizes the meaning clear light which is free of even the slightest dualistic appearance. At dawn the Buddhas give them the word empowerment elucidating the meaning clear light and the states of union. And at that very dawn they actualize the meaning clear light. Subsequently, when they rise up from it, they achieve the state of union of a trainee. In the later phase of the dawn the state of union of a trainee culminates in the state of union of a non-trainee.

WILL ALL BUDDHAS TEACH TANTRA?:

Another question that arises here is: Does this mean all future Buddhas will teach Tantra? If so, why is it said that Tantric teaching is extremely rare and Shakyamuni Buddha is one of the three among a thousand Buddhas of this aeon who taught Tantra? If not, how is it that eventually one must enter the path of Highest Yoga Tantra?

When we talk of just three out of a thousand Buddhas of this aeon teaching Tantra we are talking in terms of our world only. But according to Buddhism there are millions of other world systems too. Buddhas manifest in different world systems where they are needed. As for the Bodhisattvas on the tenth ground of the Perfection Vehicle, as residents of the Aknishta Pure Land ('og min), there is not a single moment when Buddhas are not present before them. I do not think that for them there is a dearth of Tantric teaching. What do you say?

INSTRUCTIONS ON THE MEANING CLEAR LIGHT AND THE STATES OF UNION AT DAWN:

> Should it be said that in such a case what is stated in the *Compendium of Deeds* becomes unfeasible, for it says, "Clear light is actualized at midnight." According to the import of this statement the meaning clear light is exemplified at midnight but not actualized then. It is not feasible, therefore, to assert that at midnight one arises from the meaning clear light into the body of the state of union of a trainee because in the *Clear Lamp* it is stated that the time for the initial accomplishment of a clear light must be at dawn. Also, the initial accomplishment of even the states of union of a trainee and a non-trainee must be at dawn. As the *Precious Sprout of Conclusive Analysis* (mtha' dpyod rim po che' myu gu) says, "According to the *Five Levels* (rim lnga), the *Compendium of Deeds*, and the *Drop of Liberation* (grol wa' thig le) even the state of union of a non-trainee is accomplished at dawn. This is the same time for the accomplishment of the state of union of a trainee." Also, it is not feasible to assert that the state of union of a non-trainee is actualized within the meditative equipoise of the meaning clear light at midnight without arising from it into the body of the state of union of a trainee. Unless the instructions concerning the clear light and the states of union have been given, no one can actualize the state of union of a non-trainee. If it is said that such instructions were given before the clear light at midnight, that would contradict the statement that such instructions about the meaning clear light and the states of union are given at dawn. Moreover, it is inappropriate that such instructions should be given before one has been made a suitable vessel [for the instructions] by an empowerment.

From what I have just explained to you, the meaning clear light is actualized at dawn. But some critics counter this by quoting Aryadeva's *Compendium of Deeds* which says that at midnight clear light is actualized. They take this to mean the meaning clear light, but they are

mistaken. What the statement means is that a clear light which symbolizes the meaning clear light dawns at that time but not the meaning clear
light itself. The *Clear Lamp Illuminating the Five Levels* unequivocally
states that the meaning clear light is initially actualized at dawn. As
quoted in the *Precious Sprout of Conclusive Analysis (mtha' dpyod rin po
che'i myu gu)*, the *Five Level*, the *Compendium of Deeds* and the *Drop of
Liberation*, the states of union of a trainee and a non-trainee are initially
accomplished at dawn. It is also not feasible to assert, as have some
critics, that being in meditative equipoise on the meaning clear light one
actualizes the state of union of a non-trainee at midnight. It is not
possible to actualize such a state of union without receiving instructions
on the meaning clear light and the states of union. But such instructions
could not have been given at midnight as some critics would have it,
because it is clearly stated such instructions are only given at dawn.

Concerning the attainment of the state of union of a non-trainee all
systems agree that it is attained at dawn. But, why is midnight or dawn
so crucial for actualizing the meaning clear light? As sources differ with
regard to the time when the meaning clear light is actualized, so do
scholars differ on this point. Generally speaking, it is stated in the
Tantras that the instructions on the clear light and the states of union
are given at dawn, and thereafter the clear light is also actualized
during that same dawn. But Tantric texts such as the *Compendium of
Deeds* are ambiguous on the matter. And elsewhere it is stated as if the
meaning clear light is attained at midnight. Master Yangchen Galo, the
author of this text, says that practitioners who engage in Tantric
practice from the very outset after receiving the relevant instructions,
actualize the meaning clear light at dawn; subsequently from that they
arise in the form of a pure illusory body and later achieve the state of
union of a non-trainee that same dawn. But this is not a disputed point.

Critics say that practitioners who are on the tenth ground of the
Perfection Vehicle can enter the path of Highest Yoga Tantra from the
meaning clear light of the completion stage since they attain such a clear
light at midnight during the conferral of the wisdom-knowledge empowerment. This is because they have already gained direct insight into
emptiness.

Khedrub Rinpoche in his *Commentary on the Dual Analysis (brtag
gnyis rnam bshad)* states that Bodhisattvas who are in their final lives
about to become enlightened beings are given consorts and also the
third empowerment as a substance empowerment (dngos dbang).
During the empowerment their reliance upon the vitality and exertion

of their consorts facilitates the withdrawing of winds into the central channel. As a result of this gradual dissolution of winds they experience the minds of appearance, increase and near-attainment and the three empties; following this, when they experience the clear light of great bliss and the fourth empty, such a bliss ascertains emptiness directly. This is because their earlier ascertainment of emptiness has not degenerated. According to this work, the meaning clear light is actualized at midnight when the third empowerment is given. But the instructions on the clear light and the states of union are given before the third empowerment.

Yangchen Galo disagrees with such an assertion. According to him, it is not feasible that the instructions on the clear light and the states of union would be given prior to the conferral of the third empowerment of wisdom-knowledge. That would mean that such instructions would be given before becoming a suitable recipient. Also, such a position does not stand up to analysis and reason. According to critics, the wisdom-knowledge empowerment is conferred at midnight. One experiences clear light which is preceded by the minds of three appearances and this they assert to be the meaning clear light. Here we are talking about persons who have practised the Perfection Vehicle and the three lower Tantras. Critics say that it is not necessary for them to arise in the body of a trainee; rather, within their meditative equipoise on clear light they can attain the union of a non-trainee. But according to our system such an assertion is not feasible because unless one receives instructions on the meaning clear light and the states of union it is impossible to attain them. The clear light which, according to them, is experienced at midnight is not the meaning clear light. Going by their assertion there is no opportunity for such practitioners to receive instructions on how to actualize the meaning clear light and the states of union. To say that such instructions are given before the third empowerment at mid night is invalidated by the statement of the *Clear Lamp Illuminating the Five Levels*, which clearly says that such instructions are given at dawn and the meaning clear light must initially be achieved at dawn.

How Does the Non-Trainees' State of Union Arise?:

Does the state of union of a non-trainee arise through the stirring of the wind of the meaning clear light of the final training? Or, does it arise without the stirring of such a wind?

If it is the former, it contradicts an [earlier] statement that the wind of the meaning clear light of the final trainee is not stirred. But, if it is the latter, how does one arise newly in the body of the state of union of a non-trainee, whose similar continuum did not previously exist, arising in the same way that a fish leaps from water, without even slightly stirring the wind of the meaning clear light of the final trainee? If it could arise like that, then it would undeniably follow that the state . of union of a trainee could also arise from the meaning clear light of the fourth level without its wind being stirred. The *Clear Lamp Illuminating the Five Levels* also says: "It is revealed that until the illusory body is accomplished from the mere wind and mind purified by the meaning clear light, the form body of a non-trainee will not be attained...," and also, "It should be understood as an exception that the last two levels are generated without having previously generated the levels below the illusory body of the third level..." Thus, it is stated that such a Bodhisattva has to generate the last two levels of the clear light and the state of union and then become an enlightened person [Buddha].

The critics' view is further challenged by two questions: Does the state of union of a non-trainee arise from the meaning clear light of the final level of a trainee by the stirring up of its subtle wind? Or does it arise from such a meaning clear light without the stirring up of its wind? If the critics subscribe to the former view, they contradict their earlier statement that such practitioners actualize the state of union of a non-trainee remaining in the state of meditative equipoise on the meaning clear light. If they subscribe to the latter view, then they must answer how it is that the state of union of a non-trainee arises from the meaning clear light (like a fish leaping out of water) when its continuity did not exist previously. In other words, such a state of union of a non-trainee would lack its preceding continuity of a 'similar type' (rang gi rigs 'dra snga ma) because its preceding continuity of a 'similar type' could only arise from the stirring up of the subtle wind of the meaning clear light along with the arisal of the mind of near-attainment of the reversal process. It would also be an undeniable fact [for them] that the state of union of a trainee also arises in the same way from the meaning clear light of the fourth level. According to our system a slight stirring up of the subtle wind of the meaning clear light is necessary for the arisal of the pure illusory body of such a state of union. As stated in the *Clear Lamp Illuminating the Five Levels*, it is impossible to attain the state of union of a non-trainee by just being in a state of equipoise on the meaning clear light. Many other authentic sources state that from the meaning clear light the pure illusory body is achieved together with the arisal of the mind of near-attainment of the reversal process. And the reversal process is only initiated by a slight stirring up of the subtle wind of the meaning clear light. It is this subtle wind of the subtle clear light mind which acts as the substantial cause for the pure illusory body. This fact and this process contradicts the position of critics.

> If asked, in such a case, the same text *Clear Lamp* also states, "From the spontaneously generated wisdom of the meaning clear light and the mere wind as its mount is accomplished the pure illusory body of the state of union of a non-trainee." This statement would become invalid. What this statement means is that the pure illusory body, one of the pair of the state of union of a non-trainee is accomplished from the similar continuity of the body of the state of union of a trainee that has been accomplished from the mere wind and mind of the meaning clear light.
>
> Should it be said that when Bodhisattvas, who have completed the paths of the Perfection Vehicle and the lower Tantras, eventually enter the [Highest Yoga] Tantric path they do so from the meaning clear light because they enter from the level of the meaning clear light. This thesis is not well established because the wisdom of bliss and emptiness [generated] at the time of conferring the third empowerment upon such Bodhisattvas [which exemplifies the meaning clear light preceded by the minds] of appearance, increase and near-attainment) is [also] a Tantric path [which is of the level of the meaning clear light but it is not the meaning clear light itself].

Critics quote a statement in the *Clear Lamp Illuminating the Five Levels* that one achieves the pure illusory body of the state of union of a non-trainee from the mere spontaneous wisdom of the meaning clear light and its wind. But this statement cannot be taken literally; it has to be interpreted appropriately. It cannot be taken to mean that one can attain the state of union of a non-trainee from the meaning clear light without having attained the union of a trainee. What the statement actually means is that at first one attains the state of union of a trainee and from its continuity one attains the pure illusory body which is half of a pair (the state of union of a non-`trainee), the other half being the meaning clear light.

Yogis who have completed the Perfection Vehicle or the three lower Tantras enter Highest Yoga Tantra from the level of the meaning clear light. What is meant by this is, technically speaking, they do not enter the path of Highest Yoga Tantra directly from the meaning clear light itself. As I have explained earlier, yogis on that level receive the third initiation of wisdom-knowledge at midnight at which time they experience a clear light, as wisdom of non-dual bliss and emptiness, which symbolizes the meaning clear light and this is preceded by the minds of three appearances. This path of entry is on the same level as the meaning clear light but it is not the meaning clear light. Hence, they enter Highest Yoga Tantra from the level of the meaning clear light but not from the meaning clear light itself. Later, at dawn the states of union are actualized after receiving instructions on the meaning clear light etc.

Why Must One Enter Highest Yoga Tantra:

> The reason why one must enter the path of Highest Yoga Tantra in order to achieve Buddhahood is: until the instincts of the misconception of the dualistic appearance of [the minds of] appearance, increase and near-attainment have been removed forever one will not achieve Enlightenment. The way to purify those instincts of the misconception of dualistic appearance forever so that they do not arise again is to meditate on the direct realization of suchness [emptiness] by the spontaneously generated great bliss. Such a realization is found only in the Highest Yoga Tantric Vehicle but not in other [vehicles]. Until one actualizes the meaning clear light that integrates bliss and emptiness and meditates on it, the obstructions to [omniscient] knowledge cannot be abandoned completely and therefore the Truth Body will not be attained. [Similarly] until the illusory body has been accomplished from the wind and mind purified by the meaning, clear light, the Form Body will not be achieved. Therefore, integrating bliss and emptiness and accomplishing an illusory body are the exclusive causes of the 'similar-type' required for the Truth and Form Bodies respectively, and are the innermost essence of the Highest [Yoga] Tantra

The reason why one must eventually engage in the path of Highest Yoga Tantra in order to attain enlightenment is that until and unless one removes the latent dualism of the minds of white appearance, red increase and black near-attainment it is not possible to attain Buddhahood, the supreme enlightenment. The paths of the Perfection Vehicle and the three lower Tantras do not have the power to remove such dualism. The path of Highest Yoga Tantra alone is capable of eliminating such dualism as it contains techniques to utilize fully the subtlest wind and the subtlest mind. Because of this, the spontaneous mind of great bliss can ascertain emptiness directly. Meditating (familiarizing) continually on the meaning clear light latencies of the dualistic minds of three appearances are eliminated. Unless one meditates on the meaning clear light, which naturally integrates bliss and emptiness, one will never achieve the Truth Body for the simple reason that without this clear light the obstructions to omniscience cannot be abandoned completely. And for the same reason, one will not achieve the Form Body of an enlightened being, as it has to arise from an illusory body purified by the meaning clear light.

When we speak of the meaning clear light which inseparably combines bliss and emptiness, it is extremely important for us to know what this bliss is. There are different types of bliss. For instance, one can experience a certain bliss as a result of physical and mental pliancy; such a bliss is common to Buddhists and non-Buddhists. It is neither this bliss nor the bliss of ordinary sexual union that is being referred to here. The practitioners of the completion stage enter into union with consorts which facilitates their ability to dissolve the winds into the central channel, just as these winds would dissolve at death. Alternatively through meditational practice they dissolve the winds of their bodies into the 'indestructible drop' at the heart. Either of these techniques generates the subtlest wind and subtlest mind into a spontaneous great bliss which ascertains emptiness directly; this is the non-dual bliss and emptiness of Highest Yoga Tantra. This union of the spontaneous great bliss and the meaning clear light is the uncommon substantial cause of the Truth Body. The pure illusory body which arises from the meaning clear light is the substantial cause of the Form Body. These causes are not provided by the Perfection Vehicle or the three lower Tantras for they are exclusively taught in Highest Yoga Tantra. This is primarily the reason why it is said that a practitioner has to eventually enter the path of Highest Yoga Tantra in order to achieve supreme enlightenment.

TRAINEES' STATE OF UNION:

v. The mode of transference from the meaning clear light of the fourth level to the state of union of a trainee:

The way in which one wakes up from the meaning clear light in the reversal process is as follows: As one begins to wake up from the meaning clear light its wind is slightly stirred. Simultaneously such a wind with five rays of light, which is the mount of the meaning clear light, acts as the substantial cause and the mind of clear light [itself] acts as the cooperative condition due to which [one arises as] the pure illusory body. At that time one literally accomplishes a body of 'the union with abandonment' (spangs pa dzung 'jug), which is the union of the complete abandonment of delusive obstructions and the pure illusory body, separate from the coarse body. Simultaneous with it there occurs the [mind of] near-attainment of the reversal process [which arise] from the meaning clear light, the cessation of the meaning clear light, the attainment of the liberated path of having abandoned delusive obstructions, one becomes a Foe Destroyer (Arhat), one advances to the second ground and one attains the Greater Vehicle's path of meditation.

Although at this juncture the principal state of union, the state of 'union with insight' (rtogs pa dzung 'jug), has not been achieved, nonetheless, one must consider that a state of union has been achieved. The *Clear Lamp Illuminating the Five Levels* (rim lnga gsal sgron) says: "Since there are other ways of presenting states of union, when a state of union is achieved it is not necessary that it should be presented as such a state of union (the state of union with insight)." The twenty one or twenty three states of union described in the *Five Levels* are included within the state of 'union with abandonment' and the state of 'union with insight.' And, at that time the state of 'union with abandonment' is achieved. Subsequently, the signs of the [mind of] near-attainment of the reversal process to the sign of mirage appear serially and [one wakes up] into the post meditation period.

While in the meditative equipoise on the meaning clear light of the fourth level, as soon as its subtle wind is slightly stirred one achieves the pure illusory body. The subtlest wind is its substantial cause and the meaning clear light is its cooperative condition. This wind is five coloured; the four other primary winds have colours excepting the pervasive wind. Those who have achieved the pure illusory body have completely abandoned the delusive obstructions to liberation. This state of union of a trainee comprises the pure illusory body and the factor of having abandoned all delusive obstructions. In Tibetan such a state of union is called 'spang pa dzung 'jug'. The pure illusory body is distinctively different from the old body. In such a state of meditative equipoise the illusory body can leave the old body and return to it.

Regarding the three phases of dawn: during the first phase the meaning clear light is attained; during the second phase the pure illusory body or the state of union of a trainee is attained and during the third phase the state of union of a non-trainee is attained. Although the pure illusory body can leave the old body for a hundred years, it is, however, unlikely that it would do so. Once we attain the state of union of a trainee we can attain the state of union of a non-trainee most quickly. Along with the arisal of the pure illusory body, the mind of near-attainment of the reversal process arises, the meaning clear light ceases, the liberated path of the abandonment of delusive obstructions and the second ground [of Tantra] are attained. Simultaneously, one also becomes an Arhat, the Foe Destroyer, and attains the Greater Vehicle's path of meditation. Those with the pure illusory body have attained a state of union, although they are yet to attain the principal state of 'union with insight'; in Tibetan this is called 'rtogs pa dzung 'jug'. This is because the *Clear Lamp Illuminating the Five Levels* says that apart from the way to attain the principal state of union with insight (rtogs pa dzung 'jug) there is another way to attain a state of 'union with the factor of abandonment'—'spang pa dzung 'jug'. Therefore, one could have attained a state of union other than the state of 'union with insight'.

Arya Nagarjuna in his *Five Levels* explains twenty-one or twenty-three states of union which are included in these two types of union: the state of 'union with a factor of abandonment' and the state of 'union with insight'.

I shall simply list these states of union. They are:

1. The state of union of cyclic existence and nirvana ('khor 'das zung 'jug).
2. The state of union of the afflicted class of phenomena and the liberated class of phenomena (kun byang zung 'jug).

3. The state of union of perceptions of objects with and without aspects (rnam bcas rnam med zung 'jug).
4. The state of union of subjective perception and objective phenomena (bzung 'dzin zung 'jug).
5. The state of union devoid of eternalism and nihilism (rtag chad dang bral wai' zung 'jug).
6. The state of union of emptiness and compassion (stong nyid snying rje' zung 'jug).
7. The state of union of method and wisdom (thabs shes zung 'jug).
8. The state of union of those with and those without remainder (lhag bcas lhag med kyi zung 'jug).
9. The union of the two selflessnesses (bdag med gnyis kyi zung 'jug).
10. The union of an illusory body and a clear light (sgyu lus dang 'od gsal zung 'jug).
11. The union of thorough and gradual dissolutions (ril 'dzin dang rjes gzhig gi zung 'jug).
12. The union of the two truths (bden gnyis zung 'jug).
13. The union of entering and emerging from a meditative equipoise (mnyam par 'jug ldang zung 'jug).
14. The union of sleep and wakefulness (sad gnyid zung 'jug).
15. The union of meditative equipoise and the post meditational period (mnyam rjes zung 'jug).
16. The union of mindfulness and forgetfulness (dran pa dang dran min gyi zung 'jug).
17. The union of bliss and emptiness (bde stong zung 'jug).
18. The union of objects and action (bya byed zung 'jug).
19. The union of the generation and the completion stages (skyes rdzogs zung 'jug).
20. The union of purity and impurity (dag ma dag gi zung 'jug).
21. The union of (those) with and without forms (gzugs can gzugs med kyi zung 'jug).

According to the list of twenty-two the eleventh union is divided into two and according to the list of twenty-three the fifteenth union is also divided into two.

These states of union are the divisions of the state of union of a trainee, the state of union of a non-trainee follows. It is said that even a mere understanding of a state of union is of immense benefit. The benefit is such that it is as if one has completed the coarse and the subtle levels of the generation stage. Moreover, if we aspire for such a state of union we will be likened to a person who definitely follows the path of Highest Yoga Tantra. Our womb-born human body with six constituents[63] is the best physical basis for practising Highest Yoga Tantra. We should therefore enthusiastically work for the attainment of such states of union.

A state of 'union with the factor of abandonment' of delusions is achieved when the mind of black near-attainment of the reversal process from clear light occurs. Subsequently, there arise indicative signs from the mind of red increase to the sign of mirage and then one will be in the post-meditational period.

THE MEASURE OF HAVING TRANSFERRED TO THE STATE OF 'UNION WITH INSIGHT':

> One [who has attained] the state of 'union with abandonment' once again enters into a single pointed meditative equipoise on emptiness and actualizes it by the wisdom of spontaneously generated clear light. At this point the principal state of union is achieved which is the state of union of the pure mind of the meaning clear light and the pure illusory body having the same entity/nature.

Practitioners who have abandoned completely the delusive obstructions to liberation have attained the state of 'union with the factor of abandonment' and will again enter into meditative equipoise on the meaning clear light for the sake of abandoning the obstructions to omniscient knowledge. As soon as they actualize the spontaneous wisdom of the meaning clear light they achieve the union of the pure illusory body and the meaning clear light. This is also referred to as the 'union of body and mind' which is the principal state of 'union with insight'.

THE MINDS OF THREE APPEARANCES MUST BE CONCEPTUAL:

> If anything is either [a mind of] appearance or increase or near-attainment it must be a conceptual state of mind. Though the *Combined with Sutra* (*mdo bsre*) states that [the minds of] appearance, increase and near-attainment are non-conceptual, however, this does not mean that these are not non-

conceptual minds in the sense of apprehending the objects through their generic images. The statement is made in reference to the eighty indicative conceptions; the minds [of appearance, increase and near-attainment] and the winds [as their mounts] move extremely weakly and therefore they have but slight dualistic appearances. From that point of view they [those three dualistic minds] are [just] referred to as non-conceptual [minds].

Although all the minds, even the minds of the three appearances, which dawn before the meaning clear light, are conceptual minds, there is a doubt whether or not the minds of the three appearances which dawn after the meaning clear light in the reversal process are conceptual minds. Our text dispels this doubt by stating that even the minds of three appearances of the reversal process of the meaning clear light are conceptual minds.

Arya Nagarjuna in his *Combined with Sutra* refers to the minds of the three appearances (viz., the white appearance, the red appearance and the black appearance) as non-conceptual; however, his reference has a different meaning. What he meant is compared to the eighty indicative conceptions, the minds of the three appearances are very subtle and have thus only slight dualistic appearances. Therefore, from this relative point of view, they are simply called non-conceptual. Great Nagarjuna does not mean to say that the minds of the three appearances are non-conceptual in the sense of perceiving their objects directly without the medium of a generic image.

The mind of radiant white appearance is subtler than the thirty three indicative conceptions which precede it. Similarly, the mind of radiant red increase is subtler than the forty indicative conceptions which precede it and the mind of black near-attainment is subtler than the seven indicative conceptions which precede it.[64]

The eminent scholar Ngah bdang snyan grags dpal bzang po, a throne holder, [a successor to the throne of Lama Tsongkha pa], says that [the mind of] near-attainment, just arisen from the meaning clear light of the fourth level, perceives emptiness through its [conceptual] image. But, according to Pan chen thams cad mkhyen pa blo zang dpal ldan ye shes dpal bzang po, the meaning clear light of the fourth level and [the mind of] near-attainment of the reversal process arising from it are comparable in that they both perceive the meaning of emptiness directly (dngos su) but differ in their modes of perception. As for the clear light, its mode of perception is tight due to the rapt attention paid to emptiness, whereas at the time of near-attainment the mode of perception is more relaxed due to the power of previous familiarity.

According to Trichen Ngawang Nyendak, an eminent scholar, unlike the meaning clear light, the subsequent mind of near-attainment of the reversal process ascertains emptiness through its generic image. But Panchen Lobsang Palden Yeshe disagrees with him, saying that both the meaning clear light and the subsequent mind of near-attainment of the reversal process ascertain emptiness directly. However, according to him the former's mode of ascertainment is tight whereas that of the latter is more relaxed.

THE KEY PRACTICE OF A PERSON IN THE TRAINEE'S STATE OF UNION:

If asked, what is the key-practice of a person who has (attained) the union of a trainee, the *Five Levels* (*rim lnga*) says, "Abiding in the meditative stabilization of the state of union, he/she does not train in any further [new paths]." As stated, although there is no new path in which they have to be freshly trained, however, they have to acquaint themselves further with the earlier trainings. For the purpose of abandoning obstructions to knowledge they repeatedly meditate on the 'two concentrated modes of dissolution' while abiding in the coarse body. When the time comes to accelerate their path they engage in any of the three types of conduct, due to which, according to the level of their faculties, they will see [indicative] signs for the attainment of the state of union of a non-trainee within half a month, one month or six months. They will attain the 'Eight Qualities of a Sovereign Lord' (dbang phyug gi yon tan rgyad), as stated in the *Compendium of Deeds* (*spyod bsdus*) and will also see the [indicative] signs described in the tenth analysis [chapter] of the *Samputa Tantra* (*samputa'i rgyud*). The 'Eight Qualities of a Sovereign Lord' are: subtle form, light, contact, pervasiveness, perfect attainment, great clarity, stability and control over sensual pleasures [just like] Ishvara. The 'Eight Qualities of a Sovereign Lord' and the 'Eight Sovereign Qualities'

(yon tan gyi dbang phyug rgyad) are not synonymous because the former eight are found even in the mental continuum of a person in the trainee's state of union whereas the
latter eight are qualities exclusively of a Buddha.

The key practice of those who have attained the state of union of a
trainee is to cultivate further intimacy with their path. This is what Arya
Nagarjuna has stated in his *Five Levels*. There is no new path for them to
cultivate. Since they have not abandoned the obstructions to omniscience they have to familiarize themselves further with the path that
has already been generated. In other words, for the sake of removing the
latencies of delusions they repeatedly meditate on the two modes of the
dissolution process and enter into the meaning clear light as long as
necessary.

When the time comes for them to accelerate their path they engage
in any of the 'three types of conduct' (spyod pa gsum). While engaging
in such conduct, in accordance with their different faculties, they will
see signs indicating the attainment of the state of union of a non-trainee
in fifteen days, a month or six months. The sharper the faculties the
sooner will one see such indicative signs. But within six months they
will definitely see such indicative signs.

If asked, what kind of signs do they see? They see signs associated
with their illusory body such as its subtleness, lightness and pervasiveness. It can go where ever it wishes to go. Such indicative signs are
included in the 'Eight Qualities of a Sovereign Lord' (dbang phyug gi
yon tan brgyad) mentioned in the *Compendium of Deeds*. They will also
see the signs mentioned in the tenth chapter of the *Samputa Tantra*.

We must not confuse as identical the Eight Qualities of a Sovereign
Lord (dbang phyug gi yon tan brgyad) and the Eight Sovereign Qualities (yon tan gyi dbang phyug rgyad). The former are found even in the
mindstream of those who have achieved the union of a trainee whereas
the latter are the exclusive qualities of a Buddha or completely enlightened person. These two sets of qualities are not synonymous although
the two terms sound very much alike.

CONDUCT AND ITS TYPES:

[If asked,] conduct is: a method which provides extra power
to accelerate one's practice for enhancing a meditative stabilization of bliss and emptiness by enjoying the sensual plea-

sures in general and those of a consort in particular through understanding their [true] nature.

Divisions: There are three types of conduct: a conduct with elaboration (spros bcas kyi spyod pa), a conduct without elaboration (spros med kyi spyod pa) and a conduct completely free of elaboration (shin tu spros med kyi spyod pa).

Definition of a conduct with elaboration: It is a conduct with elaboration [in the sense] that it involves an action seal [actual consort], the wearing of masks, costumes and so forth, and elaborations of activities such as gestures, reciprocal gestures, etc.

Definition of a conduct without elaboration: It is a conduct without elaboration [in the sense] that likened to the preceeding conduct, it is without elaborations of activities such as gestures and reciprocal gestures, etc.

Definition of a conduct completely free of elaborations: It is a conduct completely free of elaborations [in the sense that] without any external elaborations at all it involves an integrated meditation on the wisdom of indivisible bliss and emptiness by maintaining the clear light of sleep combined with entering into union with a wisdom seal [imagined consort].

These three include conducts of the generation stage and the completion stage as well as conducts for attaining a fresh path never achieved before and to accelerate paths which have already been achieved. Concerning the conduct without elaborations it has three types: extensive, middling and abbreviated [simple].

What is the contextual meaning of the term 'conduct' (spyod pa)? Generally speaking, it means utilizing the five sensual objects, but its contextual meaning is to be in union with a consort or consorts and experience their five sensual objects particularly the touch. The bliss of sensual touch that is experienced while in union with a consort is combined with the wisdom that ascertains her ultimate nature (i.e. emptiness of inherent existence). This enhances tremendously the experience of bliss. Alternatively speaking, a method or a technique which tremendously enhances the meditative stabilization of bliss and emptiness is referred to here as 'conduct'.

According to the *Clear Lamp* there are four occasions during which practitioners can engage in such conduct. They are:

1. On the generation stage, in order to enhance the wisdom of bliss and emptiness.
2. On the completion stage, where they have achieved the isolated mind but not an illusory body.
3. On the completion stage, where they have achieved an illusory body but not the state of union of a trainee.
4. On the completion stage, where they have attained the state of union of a trainee but not the state of union of a non-trainee. Of the 'three types of conduct' mentioned earlier, those who engage in the 'conduct with elaboration' (spros bcas kyi spyod pa), enter into union with many real consorts, such as twenty consorts, all of them wearing masks and costumes of deities. They respond with gestures, sing and dance. These ways enhance their bliss and emptiness to the state of perfection; this is the purpose of engaging in such a conduct.

Others, who engage in the 'conduct without elaboration' (spros med kyi spyod pa), enter into union with fewer real consorts (from one to five) who also wear masks and costumes of deities. This conduct is called 'without elaboration' because compared to the preceding conduct it lacks the elaborations of singing, dancing and reciprocating gestures.

And still others, who engage in the 'conduct completely free of elaboration' (shin tu spros med kyi spyod pa), forsake all the external elaborations of the preceding two types of conduct. Instead, they live in seclusion and do not seek real consorts but enter into union with a wisdom seal or a visualized consort. In their clear light of sleep they maintain the wisdom of non-dual bliss and emptiness.

These 'three types of conduct' also include the activities of practitioners on the two stages who are cultivating fresh paths not yet cultivated and accelerating the paths already cultivated.

As for the 'conduct without elaboration'; it also has three types: the elaborate, the middling and the condensed. They are distinguished from one another by taking into account, for instance, the number of consorts involved, etc.

KALACHAKRA AND OTHER HIGHEST YOGA TANTRIC SYSTEMS:

I.B. 2. e. The mode of actualizing the results:

> In general there are two systems with regard to the attainment of Buddhahood or Enlightenment by the path of Highest [Yoga Tantra] based on the aggregates of a practitioner. According to one system the aggregates [precipitated by] a ripening karmic action are exhausted by skillful means and Buddhahood is attained simultaneously. But according to the other system it is attained from within the aggregates [precipitated by such] a ripening karmic action. The former is the system of Shri Kalachakra and the latter is the system of the Highest Yoga Tantras other than Shri Kalachakra.
>
> If anyone is definitely to attain Buddhahood in one lifetime by the path of the Highest [Yoga Tantra], he/she must be a person of this continent of Jambudvipa. The attainment of Buddhahood in the intermediate state (bardo) entails accomplishing an illusory body in place of [taking birth as a being of] the intermediate state and attaining Buddhahood in that life; such a person is not of the six types of wandering beings. Those who attain Buddhahood over a succession of lives include both human beings and gods (devas).

Of the five outlines of the completion stage I shall now explain the last outline that deals with the modes of accomplishing results.

In general there are two ways by which a practitioner, depending on his or her aggregates, achieves supreme enlightenment following the paths of Highest Yoga Tantra. They are: by way of exhausting the old aggregates by skillful means and by way of retaining the old aggregates.

The first of these is, like an alchemist skillfully using elixir to change iron into gold, yogis also through skillful means exhaust their old bodies, which are precipitated by delusions and contaminated karmic actions, and thereby achieve the pure body of supreme enlightenment. This accords with the system of *Kalachakra Tantra*.[65]

The second way is to accomplish supreme enlightenment from within the old body precipitated by delusions and contaminated karmic actions. This is according to the system of Highest Yoga Tantras other than the *Kalachakra Tantra*. According to this system the old body is neither abandoned nor it is exhausted by skillful means.

The Kalachakra system explains how one's old body can be transformed into the 'Great Seal of Empty Form' (stong gdzugs phyag rgya chen po) being in union with a consort. The other system of Highest Yoga Tantras explain how to achieve the pure illusory body which will eventually become the 'Form Body'(gdzugs sku) of a Buddha.

Practitioners of the Kalachakra system arise themselves in the aspects of Kalachakra and his consort. By practising the Kalachakra the substantial particles of their bodies are exhausted and are transformed into the 'Vajra Body of Empty Form' (stong gdzugs rdo rje'i sku) and along with that their minds are transformed into the 'Supreme Immutable Bliss' (mchog tu mi 'gyur wa'i bde chen). The union of 'Empty Form' and the 'Supreme Immutable Bliss' is the union of body and mind.

According to other Highest Yoga Tantras, bliss and emptiness refer to the objective emptiness and the bliss derived from a union with consort. But in the Kalachakra system emptiness refers to the 'Empty Form' and the bliss refers to the 'Supreme Immutable Bliss'. The union of these two is also called the union of non-dual bliss and emptiness.

If asked, are the Kalachakra and other Highest Yoga Tantras incompatible for an individual practitioner? I do not think they are incompatible for a practitioner. The differences lie in the systems themselves. For instance, a Kalachakra practitioner transforms his or her body into the 'Empty Form'. Of the six subsidiary yogas, vitality and exertion allows him or her to draw the winds from the right and the left channels into the central channel and held them within it by the meditative stabilization of subsequent mindfulness and retention. Through the ignition of psychic heat (gtum mo) the white drop melts and descends till it reaches the tip of the vajra organ where it is held unreleased. In the process he or she experiences a single immutable bliss, a single substantial particle of the body is exhausted and a single negative wind is terminated. Repeating this process, he or she experiences twenty one thousand and six hundred [instances of] 'supreme immutable bliss', exhausts twenty one thousand and six hundred substantial particles of the body and terminates twenty one thousand and six hundred negative winds.

The other system of Highest Yoga Tantras says that at first one has to achieve the impure illusory body. Dissolving it into the meaning clear light of the fourth level one arises from it as the pure illusory body. This pure illusory body eventually transforms into Sambhogakaya, the Complete Enjoyment Body of the non-trainees' state of union characterized by the seven features. That is why the pure illusory body is said to be the substantial cause of Sambhogakaya.

According to the Kalachakra system the red drops are stacked from the crown of a practitioner's head to the tip of the vajra organ and the white drops are stacked up from the tip of his vajra organ to the crown of his head. There are twenty one thousand and six hundred red drops and the same amount of white drops. Due to their flow in the central channel the practitioner experiences twenty one thousand and six hundred [instances of] supreme immutable bliss, exhausts an equal number of substantial particles of his body and terminates an equal number of winds. Just as an alchemical elixir transforms iron into gold by exhausting the iron particles, this contaminated body, according to the Kalachakra system, is transformed into the 'Empty Form.' The union of this 'Supreme Immutable Bliss' and the 'Empty Form' is the non-dual bliss and emptiness of the Kalachakra system.

I feel that a practitioner cannot synthesize the Kalachakra and the system of other Highest Yoga Tantras, however, he or she can practise them alternatively.

If anyone is definitely to attain supreme enlightenment in one life by the path of Highest [Tantra] he or she must be a person of our continent (Jambudvipa).

There are those who have achieved the impure illusory body but not the supreme enlightenment in their life for they had not achieved the meaning clear light of the fourth level. At death the dissolution of their psycho-physical elements culminate in the dawning of the all-empty clear light. Subsequently, in the reversal process they attain the pure illusory body from the preceding meaning clear light. Though this happens after death in the intermediate state they are neither beings of the intermediate state (since instead of taking the form of such a being they have arisen as the pure illusory body) nor are they any of the six types of beings in cyclic existence. Thus, they achieve supreme enlightenment in the intermediate state. Earlier I have told you that according to Highest Yoga Tantras other than the Kalachakra Tantra a practitioner can achieve enlightenment within his or her body. But that was just a general statement. What I have just explained to you clearly indicates that the other Highest Yoga Tantras also assert that supreme enlightenment could be achieved even without this old body. And there are still others who can neither attain supreme enlightenment in this life nor in the intermediate state but only in successive lives. This category includes not only many of us human beings but also devas or celestial beings.

THE STATE OF UNION OF A NON-TRAINEE:

> [In this context] as a result of continuing the wholesome deeds of meditative equipoise and the post-meditational period, when persons of the trainee's state of union receive the [indicative] signs at dawn as explained before, they actualize the meaning clear light through the 'two modes of perfect realizations' (mngon par byang chub pa gnyis) induced by internal and external methods. The first instant of such a clear light is the meaning clear light of the final trainee and is equivalent to the uninterrupted path of the final life [of a Bodhisattva on the tenth ground who will become Buddha in the subsequent moment of his/her life] of the Perfection Vehicle. Thus, it acts as a direct antidote to the obstructions to knowledge and in its second moment the obstructions to knowledge are abandoned. The subsequent 'similar-type continuity' of the state of union of a trainee culminates in the body of the state of union of a non-trainee and thus, they attain the [ultimate] state of union with the seven features. From then onwards they will remain firmly for as long as cyclic existence is being emptied [of sentient beings].

Those who have already attained the state of union of a trainee, through maintaining the positive energies of both the meditational and the post-meditational periods, will see the previously mentioned signs indicating the quick attainment of the state of union of a non-trainee. Consequently, at dawn they actualize the meaning clear light by way of the 'two modes of perfect realization' induced by the internal and the external skillful methods. The two skillful methods are the external condition of a consort or consorts and the internal condition of the 'two modes of the dissolution process'. As explained earlier, the meaning clear light that is actualized is called the 'external perfect realization' since it is attained at dawn when the sky is free of the three faults— moonlight, sunlight and darkness. It is also called the 'internal perfect realization' because the meaning clear light itself is free of the minds of the three appearances.

The initial moment of this meaning clear light is the meaning clear light of the final trainee. It is equivalent to the uninterrupted path of

Bodhisattvas on the final ground of the Perfection Vehicle who will attain supreme enlightenment in the subsequent moment of that very life. This is so because they are already abiding on the direct antidote to the obstructions to omniscient knowledge. In its second moment such obstructions will have been completely abandoned and these Bodhisattvas become Buddhas. Likewise, the meaning clear light of the final trainee is the direct antidote to the obstructions to omniscient knowledge and in its subsequent moment, one achieves the state of union of a non-trainee characterized by the seven features.

The seven features (of the non-trainee's state of union) such as embracing each other are as explained by Acharya Ngawang Drakpa. They are:

1. Complete Enjoyment Body.
2. Embracing each other.
3. Great bliss.
4. Lack of inherent existence.
5. Filled with compassion.
6. Uninterrupted continuity.
7. Non-cessation.

ENLIGHTENED BODIES:

The objective clear light characterized by such dual purities is the 'Non-Composite Truth Body' and the subjective clear light is the 'Wisdom Truth Body', also known as the 'Body of Great Bliss'. Their basis, a 'Form Body' accomplished from mere wind and mind, is the 'Enjoyment Body'. The Truth and Form Bodies are of the same nature and differ only nominally. Hence, the Form Body is called the 'Non-dual Wisdom Body'.

The emptiness of the mind of great bliss of the state of union of a non-trainee is referred to as the objective clear light characterized by dual purities as follows. It's nature is primordially pure and it is also pure of adventitious defilements. It is the unproduced Natural Truth Body. The subjective clear light which perceives it, is the Wisdom Truth Body or the Great Bliss Body.

The Form Body which is the basis of the other two bodies is accomplished from the most subtle wind and mind. It is the Complete Enjoyment Body. The Truth and Form Bodies have the same nature but differ nominally. For this reason the Form Body is also called the Non-dual Wisdom Body.

> Acharya Gandapada asserts the wisdom of great bliss and
> the state of union of non-trainees as the 'Natural Truth
> Body'. For this reason, according to this system, every [in-
> stance] of a 'Natural Truth Body' does not necessarily have to
> be a true cessation and a non-composite [phenomenon]. It is
> also said that the vase empowerment, secret empowerment
> and wisdom-knowledge empowerment can accomplish the
> three Vajras—the Vajra Body, Vajra Speech, and Vajra Mind
> or the Emanation Body, the Enjoyment Body and the Truth
> Body. It follows from this that the mere general 'Form Body'
> is the 'Emanation Body,' Buddha's speech is the 'Enjoyment
> Body', and his mind is the 'Truth Body'. If so, could one say
> that the 'Enjoyment Body' characterized by the major and
> the minor marks and which is said to be accomplished by the
> vase empowerment is an 'Emanation Body'. In general,
> however, it is not to be accepted as an 'Emanation Body', so
> research is needed to be done on this point.

But according to Acharya Gandhapada the wisdom of great bliss and the state of union of a non-trainee are the Natural Truth Body. That is why, according to the Tantric system, if anything is a Natural Truth Body it is not necessary that it should be a true cessation. The wisdom of great bliss and the state of union of a non-trainee are not true cessations or unproduced phenomena. Contrarily, according to the Perfection Vehicle if anything is a Natural Truth Body then it must necessarily be a true cessation and an unproduced phenomenon. For this reason, the Perfection Vehicle asserts the objective emptiness of the blissful omniscient mind characterized by the dual purities as the Natural Truth Body but not the subjective blissful omniscient mind itself.

It is explained that the three Vajras of the body, speech and mind of an enlightened being are achieved through the vase, the secret and the wisdom-knowledge empowerments. The vase empowerment purifies the stains and faults of ordinary appearance and ordinary clinging to the body; it empowers us to meditate on the generation stage. This empowerment plants in us the seeds/potency to eventually achieve the resultant Emanation Body. Here the term 'Emanation Body' is used liberally to include even the Complete Enjoyment Body.

The secret empowerment plants in us the seeds to attain the Complete Enjoyment Body. Here it refers to the speech of a Buddha.

The wisdom-knowledge empowerment plants in us the seeds to accomplish the Truth Body, which refers to the omniscient mind of a Buddha. Generally when we talk about the 'Three Kayas' or the three bodies of a Buddha, the Emanation Body and the Complete Enjoyment Body are counted separately. But in the context of the vase empowerment even the Complete Enjoyment Body characterized by thirty two noble signs and eighty auspicious signs is taken for an Emanation Body. In this regard, our author wonders if we could say that this Emanation Body accomplished by the vase empowerment is not the same Emanation Body counted in the general list of the three enlightened bodies.

Part Four:
The Ten Grounds and the Five Paths:

II. The mode of establishing the ten grounds etc., and the five paths:

A. How Tantras and commentarial treatises present them.
B. Presentation of Summary.

II.A. How Tantras and commentarial treatises present them:

In the Perfection Vehicle it is said that there are ten grounds of superior (Arya) trainees, from the first ground of the Very Joyous to the tenth ground, the Cloud of Dharma. If the Omnipresent Light, the ground of non-trainees, is added to them, then, there are eleven grounds. [Also], if the ground of Aspiring Activity (mos pa spyod pa' sa) of an ordinary person is added to them there are twelve [grounds]. There is mention of two grounds of an ordinary person—the ground of Aspiring Activity and the ground of a Beginner (las dang po pa' sa)—in some texts.

According to the presentation of grounds in the system of Highest [Yoga] Tantra, [differing] numbers of grounds are mentioned in the root and explanatory Tantras and commentarial treatises, as follows: ten, eleven, twelve, thirteen, fourteen, fifteen and even sixteen. The names given to the grounds and so forth agree in some cases but not in others. In the eleventh chapter of the *Guhyasamaja Root Tantra* (*gsang 'dus rtsa rgyud*) it is said, "They will become Bodhisattvas; Abiding on the ten grounds." Thus, it just mentions the ten grounds. The *Bright Lamp* (*sgron gsal*) explains these grounds in the light of the ten winds.

The *Explanatory Tantra Vajra Garland* (*bshad rgyud rdo rje 'phreng wa*) says: "Each of the eleven vase empowerments and the three higher empowerments, fourteen in all, is a ground in itself." Except for the mention of these fourteen grounds, neither their names nor their meanings are clearly elucidated.

Generally speaking, according to the Perfection Vehicle there are ten grounds of Arya Bodhisattvas or Superior trainees, from the Very Joyous (rab dga') to the Cloud of Dharma (chos kyi sprin). When the Omnipresent Light of Buddha or the non-trainee is added to them it is the eleventh ground. Sometimes the ground of ordinary beings called the Aspiring Activity (which includes both the path of accumulation and the path of preparation) is added to them, then, there are twelve grounds. If this ground of ordinary beings is split into two as some sources do, then the fresh attainment of the path of accumulation is called the ground of a beginner. With this new addition to the list of twelve, then there are thirteen grounds.

We can find the presentation of the grounds of Highest Yoga Tantra in the *Root Tantra*, the *Explanatory Tantras* and their commentarial treatises. A varying number of grounds is mentioned in them, from ten to fourteen to even sixteen. Concerning the names of the grounds in some sources they accord with each other but in others they do not.

The eleventh chapter of the *Guhyasamaja Root Tantra* simply mentions that there are ten grounds on which Bodhisattvas abide by. In the *Clear Lamp* these ten grounds are explained as referring to the ten winds. The ten winds are grouped into two—the primary winds and the secondary winds. The five primary winds are: the Life Sustaining wind, the Downward Voiding wind, the Upward Moving wind, the Equally Abiding wind, and the Pervasive wind. The five secondary winds are: the Moving wind, the Thoroughly Moving wind, the Rapidly Moving wind, the Perfectly Moving wind and the Definitely Moving wind.

Among the six explanatory Tantras of Guhyasamaja, the explanatory Tantra *Vajra Garland* (rdo rje 'phreng wa) says that each of the eleven vase empowerments and the three higher empowerments is a ground. The eleven vase empowerments are: water, crown, bell, vajra, name, mantra, prophecy and giving relief, vajra discipline, disciplined conduct, irreversible vajra acharya empowerment, and subsequent permission. The three higher empowerments are the secret empowerment, the wisdom-knowledge empowerment and the word empowerment. Excepting the mention of these fourteen grounds, neither their names nor a clear exposition is given on them.

The [Explanatory Tantra] *Prophetic Revelation of Thought* (*dgongs pa lung ston*) says: "That on which Buddhas are; Is the thirteenth ground." Except for the mention of the meaning clear light of the fourth level as the thirteenth ground neither the names of grounds nor their meanings are given.

The *Five Levels* (*rim lnga*) says: "The eighth ground is attained by the practice of preliminary activity (dang po las kyi sbyor wa). And the seers of the three appearances firmly abide on the tenth ground." Also, the *Compendium of Deeds* (*spyod bsdus*) says: "According to the Vajra Vehicle, by practising the generation stage the eighth ground is attained. [But] the tenth ground is attained by way of a clear realization of the body, speech and mind." These two texts are in accord in saying that the practice of preliminary activity (i.e. the generation stage) is the eight ground and seeing the three appearances (a clear realization of the body, speech and mind), which is the isolated mind, corresponds to the tenth ground.

In the *Root and Explanatory [Guhyasamaja] Tantras* as well as in the tradition of the Arya father [Nagarjuna] and [his spiritual] sons, the presentation of the grounds is not explained further than that.

The *Prophetic Revelation of Thought* (*dgongs pa lung ston*), another explanatory Tantra of Guhyasamaja, also simply mentions the meaning clear light of the fourth level as the thirteenth ground; apart from this it neither provides the names of the grounds nor an explanation.

Great Nagarjuna in his *Five Levels* states that by the Preliminary Activity (las kyi sbyor wa) one attains the eighth spiritual ground and the others who have seen the three appearances firmly abide on the tenth ground.

Aryadeva, his chief disciple, states in his *Compendium of Deeds* (*spyod sdus*) states that by practising the generation stage of the Vajra Vehicle one attains the eighth ground and through the clear realization of the body, speech and mind, which is isolated mind, one attains the tenth ground. In this respect the *Five Levels* and the *Compendium of Deeds* agree with each other. They both assert that by the Preliminary Activity (las kyi sbyor va) one attains the generation stage and through the realizations of the isolated body, the isolated speech and the isolated mind of the completion stage one attains the tenth ground. This is the ending of the presentation of the grounds in the *Root* and the *Explanatory Tantras of Guhyasamaja* (*gsang 'dus rtsa bshad kyi rgyud*) as well as the treatises of Arya Nagarjuna and his spiritual sons such as Aryadeva, Acharya Nagabodhi, Acharya Shakyamitra, Acharya Chandrakirti and others. The *Root Tantra* has eighteen chapters of which the first seventeen are the *Root* and the eighteenth is referred to as the *Subsequent Tantra*.

> The *Hevajra Tantra* (*kye rdor gyi rgyud*) and the fifth Analysis [chapter] of the *Samputa Tantra* say: "These are the twelve grounds: the Seat and the Adjacent Seat, likewise the Field and the Adjacent Field, Chandoha ('dun rtog) and the Adjacent Chandoha (nye wa'i 'dun rtog), likewise the Gathering and the Adjacent Gathering, the Cemetery and the Adjacent Cemetery, Pilava (thung gcod) and the Adjacent Pilava (nye wa'i thung gcod)." Thus, they mention these twelve grounds, whose names do not accord with those of the Perfection Vehicle.
>
> In the same Analysis (chapter) of *Samputa [Tantra]* and in the fiftieth chapter of the *Chakrasamvara Root Tantra* ('khor lo bde mchog gi rtsa rgyud) it is said, "The Seat is the Very Joyous ground; likewise, Adjacent Seat is the Stainless, the Field should be understood here as the Illuminating, the Adjacent Field is the Radiant, Chandoha is the Difficult to Overcome, the Adjacent Chandoha is the Manifest/Approaching (mngon du gyur wa), the Gathering is the Gone Afar, the Adjacent Gathering is the Unshakable, the Cemetery is the Good Intelligence, and the Adjacent Cemetery is the Cloud of Dharma." In this way the Seat and so forth are said to be the ten grounds. Although it appears in texts such as the *Samputra [Tantra]* and the *Unsurpassed Clear Expression* (mngon brjod bla ma) that the Chando is the Manifest/Approaching (mngon du gyur wa) and the Adjacent Chando is the Difficult to Overcome, commenting on this, the seventeenth cluster [chapter] of the *Cluster of Quintessential Instructions* (man ngag snye ma' snye ma bcu bdun pa) says: "Yearning Conception ('dun rtog) is the Very Difficult to Overcome...," and, "...the Adjacent Yearning Conception (is attained) by the Manifest/Approaching." This should be accepted as it stands because the 'Chando' of 'Chandoha' refers to 'Yearning' and 'uha'

refers to 'Conception.' The same text (*Cluster*) says, "Pilava ('thung gchod) is the ground of Aspiring Activity (mos pa spyod pa' sa) and the twelfth ground, Omnipresent Light, is the Adjacent Pilava." Thus, 'Pilava' is described as the ground of Aspiring Activity and the 'Adjacent Pilava' as the Omnipresent Light ground.

The *Hevajra Tantra* (*kye rdor rgyud*) and the fifth Analysis (chapter) of the *Samputa Tantra* present twelve grounds whose names are very different from the names of the grounds in the Perfection Vehicle. They are: Seat, Adjacent Seat, Field, Adjacent Field, Chandoha, Adjacent Chandoha, Gathering, Adjacent Gathering, Cemetry, Adjacent Cemetry, Pilava/Drinking Cutting (thung gcod) and Adjacent Pilava/Drinking Cutting (nye wa'i thung gcod). The fifth Analysis of the *Samputa Tantra* and the fiftieth chapter of the *Chakrasamvara Root Tantra* correlate those grounds to the ten grounds such as Very Joyous of the Perfection Vehicle serially.

Sources such as the *Unsurpassable Clear Expression* (*mgnon brjod bla ma*) and the *Samputa Tantra* mention Chando as the Manifest/Approaching (mngon du gyur wa) ground and the Adjacent Chando as the Difficult to Overcome. Commenting on this, the seventeenth chapter of the *Cluster of Quintessential Instruction* (*man ngag snye ma*) explains the meaning of the word 'Chandoha'. It says that 'Chand' of 'Chandoha' means 'Yearning' ('dun pa) and 'uha' means 'Conception' (rtog pa). Thus, it means 'Yearning Conception' ('dun rtog). It states that the 'Yearning Conception' ('dun rtog) is the 'Very Difficult to Overcome' and the Manifest/Approaching (mngon du gyur wa) leads to the Adjacent Yearning Conception (nye wa'i 'dun rtog). According to our text we should follow this latter presentation. Also the *Cluster of Quintessential Instruction* correlates the last two grounds of the *Hevajra Tantra* to the ground of Aspiring Activity and the Omnipresent Light of the Perfection Vehicle. It says Pilava or Drinking Cutting (thung gcod) is the Aspiring Activity and the Adjacent Pilava (nye wa'i thung gcod) is the twelfth ground which is called the Omnipresent Light. The Aspiring Activity is the path of preparation with its four levels, which is taken as the first ground.

The *Ornament of Vajra Essence Tantra* (*rdo rje snying po rgyan gyi rgyud*) mentions twelve grounds with different names, from "the great ground of Omnipresent Light" (kun tu 'od) to "the twelfth [ground of] Self-Awareness (so so bdag rig pa)." They are: the Omnipresent Light, Nectar Light, Space Light, Vajra Light, Jewel Light, Lotus Holder, Action Light, Without Example (dpe med pa), Devoid of Example (dpe dang bral wa), Wisdom Light, Omniscient One and the Self-Knower/Apperception. The thirtieth chapter of the *Unsurpassed Clear Expression* (*mngon brjod bla ma*) mentions thirteen grounds. It states, "The twelve grounds are as follows: [Adding] "Without Example (dpe med pa) and Possessing Wisdom (ye shes ldan) to the ten grounds such as the 'Very Joyous and the Stainless.' The Vajra ground is the thirteenth."

The *Ornament of Vajra Essence Tantra* (*rdo rje snying poi' rgyan gyi rgyud*) also presents twelve grounds with different names but they are the same grounds as in the Perfection Vehicle and the *Samputa Tantra*. The twelve grounds are: Omnipresent Light, Nectar Light, Space Light, Vajra Light, Jewel Light, Lotus Holder, Action Light, Without Example (dpe med pa), Devoid of Examples (dpe dang bral wa), Wisdom Light, Omniscience, and Individual Self Knower/Apperception.

The thirtieth chapter of the *Unsurpassable Clear Expression* presents thirteen grounds, adding three more to the ten grounds of the Perfection Vehicle from Very Joyous to the Cloud of Dharma. They are: Without Example (the eleventh ground), Endowed with Wisdom (the twelveth ground) and Vajra ground (the thirteenth).

The second chapter of the *Drop of Mahamudra—the Great Seal* (*phyag chen thig le*) says: "The Acharya [master] empowerment is classified as the eleventh; the secret empowerment as the twelfth; the wisdom-knowledge as the thirteenth; and the [word of] suchness as the fourteenth. Each empowerment is a ground and those [who have received these empowerments] are the lords of the grounds." What is said here accords with *Vajra Garland* (*rdor rje phreng wa*).

The eighteenth chapter of the *Drop of Exalted Wisdom* (*ye shes thig le*) says: "The first is the ground of Aspiring Activity, the second is Very Joyful, the third is Stainless, the fourth is Luminous, the fifth is Radiant, the sixth is Difficult to Overcome, the seventh is Manifest/Approaching, the eight is Gone Afar, the ninth is Unshakable, and the tenth is Good Intelligence. These are the grounds of Bodhisattvas. The

Cloud of Dharma is the ground of a Buddha. The Omnipresent Light (kun tu 'od) is the ground of a perfectly accomplished Buddha. The All Illuminating Light (kun tu snang wa mched pa'i 'od) is the ground of an Emanation Body of the glorious Bhagawan Vajrasattva. The Light of All Illuminating Attainment (kun tu snang wa thob pa'i 'od) is the ground of a Complete Enjoyment Body. The Inexpressible and Immeasurable (brjod du med pa tshad med pa) is the ground of Great Bliss. It is stated thusly, "These are all instances of joy (bliss); Intellectually imputed as grounds." The same [text] also says: "The eleventh ground is perpetually recalled (dran pa) as the Emanation Body, the twelfth as the Enjoyment Body and the thirteenth as the Truth Body. The fourteenth is Great Bliss and the fifteenth is called the ground of Exalted Wisdom. But, the sixteenth is left unimputed."

The Very Joyous to the Cloud of Dharma are the grounds of a trainee and the subsequent grounds are the grounds of a non-trainee. Some scholars also say that the tenth ground is that of a Buddha. However, it is not the ground of a perfectly accomplished Buddha. The grounds such as Without Example are the divisions within the eleventh ground, which is called Omnipresent Light.

The second chapter of the *Drop of Mahamudra—the Great Seal* (*phyag chen thig le*) mentions fourteen grounds which correspond to those of the *Vajra Garland*. Each of the fourteen empowerments is considered as an individual ground. The Vajra Acharya (master) empowerment, which is the eleventh ground, is split into three: the secret empowerment (the twelfth ground), the wisdom-knowledge empowerment (the thirteenth ground) and the word empowerment (the fourteenth ground).

The eighteenth chapter of the *Drop of Wisdom* (*ye shes thig le*) has a slightly different way of listing the grounds. It says that from the ground of Aspiring Activity to the Good Intelligence are the grounds of Bodhisattvas whereas the Cloud of Dharma is the ground of a Buddha. Furthermore, it says that Omnipresent Light (the eleventh ground) is the ground of a perfectly accomplished Buddha, All Illuminating Light (the twelfth ground) is the ground of the Glorious Emanation Body Bhagawan Vajrasattva, Light of All Illuminating Attainment (the thirteenth ground) is the ground of the Complete Enjoyment Body, Inexpressible and Immeasurable (the fourteenth ground) is the ground of

Great Bliss, and Wisdom ground is the fifteenth ground. But the sixteenth ground is left unnamed. All these grounds are just the divisions of joy or the great bliss simply imputed as grounds.

> The ground of Aspiring Activity is a ground of ordinary beings since it is explained as referring to the four levels of the path of preparation, such as the heat level. The remainders are the grounds of Superiors (Aryas). It is stated further that although the tenth ground, the Cloud of Dharma, is called a ground of Buddha, it is not the ground of a perfectly accomplished Buddha. This is in accordance with the intention of the *Wisdom Gone Beyond Sutras* (*sher phyin gyi mdo*) and also the *Ornament for Clear Realization* (*mrngon rtogs rgyan*). On the other hand, if the ground of Aspiring Activity is taken as the first [ground] then the Cloud of Dharma becomes the eleventh ground.

The ground of Aspiring Activity is an ordinary ground because it is the path of preparation with its four levels. The four levels are the Heat, Peak, Patience and Supreme Dharma. The remaining grounds such as Joyous are the grounds of Aryas or Superiors who have gained direct insight into emptiness. According to the *Ornament for Clear Realization* and the *Wisdom Gone Beyond Sutras* the tenth ground, the Cloud of Dharma, is simply called the ground of a Buddha. It is not the ground of a fully enlightened person—a real Buddha.

> But, if the Omnipresent Light is divided into four—the three [Buddha's] bodies and the body of Great Bliss and each ground counted individually, then there are fifteen grounds. Alternatively, taking the Very Joyful as the first [ground] and counting the three bodies, the Great Bliss Body and the Exalted Wisdom Body individually as grounds there are fifteen grounds. However, if the ground of Aspiring Activity is taken as the first [ground] then, there are sixteen grounds. For this reason, a commentary to the *Drop of Exalted Wisdom* also mentions sixteen grounds. Hence, it is not as if this system does not accept more than fifteen grounds.

According to both the Perfection and the Tantric vehicles, all the bodies of a Buddha—an enlightened being—are achieved simultaneously. This means that all the grounds of a non-trainee are also achieved simultaneously. Whether there are fifteen grounds or sixteen grounds, the latter grounds such as the three bodies of an enlightened person as individual grounds are the divisions within the blissful omniscient wisdom.

According to the Perfection Vehicle, Bodhisattvas on the tenth ground who will achieve supreme enlightenment in their final life will have to take rebirth in Aknishta ('og min)—the Pure Celestial Environment Below None—and there they will become enlightened beings. Their emanations in other worlds such as our's will attain enlightenment simultaneously with them. Remaining in the state of a Complete Enjoyment Body they can send forth emanations to other worlds to promote the welfare of sentient beings.

B. Presentation of a summary:

> As stated earlier, the ten grounds as presented in Tantric texts such as the *Root Text of Heruka Tantra* and the *Sambhuta Tantra* are as follows: "[From] the Seat as the Very Joyous ground to the Adjacent Cemetery as the Cloud of Dharma." These are the ten grounds of a superior (Arya) trainee. There are two views as to whether or not the names of [such grounds] accord with the names of [the grounds of] the Perfection Vehicle. Notwithstanding that, it should be known that these two views are the same as far as the meaning is concerned.

The varying number of grounds in both the Perfection Vehicle and Highest Yoga Tantra is just a matter of classification; they do not contradict one another. If the Very Joyous is taken as the first ground then the tenth ground would be the Cloud of Dharma; but if the Aspiring Activity is taken as the first ground then the Cloud of Dharma would be the eleventh ground. In addition to them, if the ground of Omnipresent Light is divided into the three bodies of a Buddha and the body of great bliss, then, there are fifteen grounds. Or if the ground of Omnipresent Light is divided into five bodies—the Truth Body, the Complete Enjoyment Body, the Emanation Body, the Great Bliss Body and the Exalted Wisdom Body—and added to the ten grounds from the Very Joyous to the Cloud of Dharma, there are fifteen grounds. If the ground of Aspiring Activity is added to them as the first ground, then there are sixteen grounds. A commentary to the *Drop of Exalted Wisdom* does mention sixteen grounds. Various sources classify grounds differently; for this reason texts speak of ten, eleven, twelve, thirteen, fourteen, fifteen and even sixteen grounds. The ten grounds of Superior trainees mentioned in the *Heruka Root Tantra* and the *Samputa Tantra* are the ten grounds of the Perfection Vehicle with different names such as Seat and Adjacent Seat. The ten grounds of the Perfection Vehicle are correlated with the ten perfections from generosity to exalted wisdom. Also, according to the Perfection Vehicle, Bodhisattvas on the ten grounds specialize in a particular perfection (e.g. generosity on the first ground); for this reason they have developed a special ability in that particular perfection. But that does not mean they do not practise other perfections. Most amazingly, they practise all other perfections within each perfection.

If asked, "Is there any reason for the names given to various grounds in the Tantric system?" "Yes, There is." The first ground is called 'seat' because, figuratively speaking, it is like sitting on a seat where one experiences tremendous joy from satisfying others' needs through gifts. Just to hear anyone asking for a gift brings infinite joy or happiness to such a practitioner. The words, `Give me' has become a magic word for those on the first ground.

The second ground is called 'adjacent seat' because of its being adjacent or close to the preceding ground with which it also has a cause and effect relationship.

The third ground is called 'field' because it is like a field which brings forth the crops of patience and other qualities such as the clairvoyances.

The fourth ground is called 'adjacent field' because of its being adjacent or close to the preceding ground with which it also has a cause and effect relationship.

The fifth is called 'chandoha' ('dun rtog) because of the yearning conception to endow others with all wonderful things.

The sixth ground is called 'adjacent chandoha' (nye wa'i 'dun rtog) because of its being adjacent or close to the preceding ground with which it also has a cause and effect relationship.

The seventh is called 'gathering' for the reason that one is able to gather meditative stablization and clairvoyance in one's mindstream. Alternatively speaking, in the case of Heruka practitioners they generate sixty two deities on their bodies and then gather (invite) the deities of the twenty four sacred places of Heruka on this earth to dissolve them into the deities of their body mandala.

The eigth ground is called 'adjacent gathering' because of its being adjacent or close to the preceding ground with which it also has a cause and effect relationship. On this ground Bodhisattvas have gained special power over aspirational prayers.

The ninth ground is called 'cemetery', here Bodhisattvas have achieved special ability in the perfection of power: the corpse-like two misconceptions of the self are cremated in the cemetry of the two selflessnesses.

The tenth ground is called 'adjacent cemetery' because of its being adjacent or close to the preceding ground with which it also has a cause and effect relationship.

As we have seen, some tantric texts refer to the ten grounds by the same names as the Perfection Vehicle but others have different names for them. Notwithstanding such a superficial difference, the grounds are the same in all.

As stated in tantric sources such as *Samputra Tantra* the ten grounds according to the tantric system are the grounds of a Superior (Arya) trainee. But their names such as Seat and Adjacent Seat as mentioned in the *Hevajra Tantra* and the *Samputa Tantra* are very different from those of the Perfection Vehicle. The *Ornament of the Vajra Essence Tantra* also has very different names for the grounds, such as Nectar Light. According to the *Great Exposition of the Stages of Mantra* and *Elucidation of All Hidden Meanings (sbas don kun gsal)* notwithstanding the different names given to the grounds, all such sources are speaking about the same grounds but following different modes of classification.

PRESENTING ELEVEN AND TWELVE GROUNDS:

> The mode of establishing eleven grounds is: adding the Omnipresent Light, the ground of Buddha, to those ten grounds. As the *Second Cluster* (the second chapter of the *Cluster of the Quintessential Instructions (man ngag snye ma)* says: "Because of their being the bases for higher qualities they should be seen as the eleven grounds, from the Very Joyous to the Cloud of Dharma to the Omnipresent Light."
>
> The twelve grounds are those eleven grounds with the addition of the ground of Aspiring Conduct as the first. In the *Hevajra* and the *Sambuta [Tantras]* they were given names from the Seat to the Adjacent Pilava. As the *Hevajra [Tantra]* says, "Those are the twelve grounds. *The Great Exposition of the Stages of Tantra (snags rim chen mo)* and the *Elucidation of All Hidden Meanings (sbas don kun gsal)* comment on this

statement and also the twelve grounds using different names, such as the Omnipresent Light and the Nector Light, as mentioned in the *Ornament of the Vajra Essence Tantra* (*rdo rje snying po rgyan gyi rgyud*), stating that these grounds can be corelated to the previous twelve grounds sequentially.

There are different ways of listing the grounds. The way to establish eleven grounds is to add, as stated in the *Second Cluster* (*snye ma gnyis pa*), the ground of a Buddha to the ten grounds from Very Joyous to the Cloud of Dharma. And the way to establish twelve grounds is to add the ground of Aspiring Activity to the eleven grounds. The *Hevajra Tantra, Samputa Tantra* and the *Ornament of the Vajra Essence Tantra* give different names to the grounds.

PRESENTING THIRTEEN GROUNDS:

There are two ways mentioned in the *Cluster of Quintessential Instructions* (*man snyer*) for presenting thirteen grounds. Firstly, the ground of ordinary persons is divided into two— the ground of Beginners and the ground of Aspiring Activity—to which are added the eleven grounds such as the Very Joyous, as mentioned earlier. Secondly, as stated in the *Unsurpassed Clear Expression*, added to the ten grounds such as the Very Joyous are the ground Without Example [having the nature of a special path,] the ground Endowed With Wisdom [having the nature of an uninterrupted path] and the Vajra ground [having the nature of the Omnipresent Light]. [To substantiate these points] the *Second Cluster* says, "Therefore, the eleven grounds, with the [addition of the] ground of Aspiring Activity, become twelve and together with the Beginner's ground become thirteen, or with the [addition of the] ground Without Example [having the nature of a special path] become twelve and together with the ground Endowed With Wisdom (having the nature of an uninterrupted path of the ground of Buddha] become thirteen." Of these the first [ground of Beginners and Aspiring Activity] is presented as a common ground of both the ordinary persons and the Superior [beings] whereas the subsequent ones are presented exclusively as the grounds of the Superiors (Aryas). According to the *Unsurpassed Clear Expression*, the tenth ground is divided into three: the usual tenth ground or the Freshly Attained tenth ground, the ground Without Example [which is a special path of the tenth ground], and the ground Endowed With Wisdom [the uninterrupted path of the final continuum of a person on the tenth ground who will attain Buddhahood in the subsequent moment of his/her life].

There are two ways to establish thirteen grounds. One way, as stated in the *Cluster of Quintessential Instruction*, is to add Beginners' ground (which is the path of accumulation) and the ground of Aspiring Activity (which is the path of preparation with its four levels) to the eleven grounds from Very Joyous to the ground of a Buddha. The other way, as stated in the *Unsurpassed Clear Expression*, is to add three more to the ten grounds: the ground Without Example having the nature of a special path; this is the fresh attainment of the tenth ground since the tenth ground is divided into three, and the ground Endowed with Wisdom having the nature of the uninterrupted path, the second level of the tenth ground, and the Vajra ground having the nature of All Pervading Light, which is the uninterrupted path of a final trainee that will transform into the Omniscient wisdom in its subsequent moment.

According to the *Cluster* (*snye ma*), of the thirteen grounds the first two are common grounds of both Ordinary persons and Superiors (Arya), whereas remaining eleven are the exclusive grounds of Superiors. However, all the thirteen grounds presented in the *Unsurpassed Clear Expression* are the exclusive grounds of Superiors. This is because the tenth ground is divided into three grounds—the Tenth (usual), Without Example, and Endowed with Wisdom.

The meaning clear light of the fourth level is described as the thirteenth ground in the [Explanatory Tantra] *Prophetic Revelation of the Thought* (*dgongs pa lung ston*). It is presented as the thirteenth ground in the context of dividing each of the four levels of the path of preparation into three [levels] such as the small, the middling and the great. Thus there are twelve grounds, as described in a commentary to the *Compendium of Deeds* and also in some commentaries to the *Five Levels*. As the commentary to the *Compendium of Deeds* says, "...from reaching the final [level of] heat to the patience and the supramundane [levels], there are twelve [levels] of the [path of] preparation, such as the middling and the great. The Very Joyous is the thirteenth [ground]." With reference to this, it should be understood that the state of union of a trainee is presented as the fourteenth ground.

The mode of presenting the path of preparation in twelve grounds is as follows: According to the same commentary [on the *Compendium of Deeds*] through the Vajra Recitation one attains the middling and the great [levels] of the 'patience level' of the path of preparation, [which are] the eighth ground. Through the isolated mind, one attains the small and the middling [levels] of the 'supramundane qualities'. Through the illusory body, one achieves the great [level] of the 'supramundane qualities'. Therefore, it must be asserted that by the generation stage one attains these seven [levels]: the small, the middling and the great [levels] of the 'heat level' of the path of preparation, the small, the middling and the great levels of its 'peak level', and the small level of its 'patience' [level]. Alternatively according to the *Compendium of Deeds*, in the *Prophetic Revelation of the Thought* isolated mind is correlated with the tenth ground; hence, illusory body is the eleventh ground and the meaning clear light is the twelfth ground. However, when the [ground of] Aspiring Activity is taken as the first [ground], then the meaning clear light is established as the thirteenth [ground].

According to the *Explanatory Tantra Prophetic Revelation of Thought* the meaning clear light of the fourth level is the thirteenth ground when the four levels of the path of preparation are divided in to twelve grounds.

A commentary on the *Compendium of Deeds* and the *Five Levels* divide each of the four levels of the path of preparation into three sub-levels: the small, the middling and the great. Each of these twelve levels of the path of preparation is treated as an individual ground. Added to them is the Very Joyous ground which is the meaning clear light. From this point of view it can be said that the state of union of a non-trainee is the fourteenth ground. In the Perfection Vehicle one achieves the path of seeing as soon as one experiences a direct insight into emptiness. This direct insight into emptiness according to Highest Yoga Tantric system is the meaning clear light. Of the twelve levels of the path of preparation the first seven are achieved by the generation stage; the eighth and the ninth by the Vajra Recitation or the isolated speech; the tenth and the eleventh by the isolated mind and the twelfth by the illusory body.

Another interpretation of the statement in the *Prophetic Revelation of Thought* according to the *Compendium of Deeds* is this that isolated mind is the tenth ground, illusory body is the eleventh and meaning clear light is the twelfth. But, counting from the Aspiring Activity as the first then meaning clear light becomes the thirteenth ground.

PRESENTING FOURTEEN GROUNDS:

> The mode of establishing the fourteen grounds is as follows: according to the *Vajramala (rdo rje phreng wa)* and the *Drop of Mahamudra—the Great Seal (phyag chen thig le)*, each of the fourteen empowerments is correlated with a ground. The fourteen empowerments are: the eleven vase empowerments—water, crown, vajra, bell, name, mantra empowerment, prophecy and [giving] relief combined as one, vajra discipline, behavourial discipline, irreversible vajra acharya empowerment, subsequent permission, and the three higher empowerments—secret empowerment, wisdom-knowledge empowerment and the fourth empowerment (the word empowerment). The fourteen correlative grounds are the thirteen grounds, as mentioned in the *Unsurpassed Clear Expression,* with the addition of Aspiring Activity as the first.
>
> If asked,"What does it mean that the fourteen empowerments are correlated with fourteen grounds," because it would be extremely absurd to say that they are equivalent substitutes (dod thub). The *Clear Lamp Illuminating the Five Levels (rim lnga gsal sgron)* says that they are correlated from the point of view of a single concomitant factor. But, in many other texts it is stated that it is as fortunate to receive these empowerments as it is to attain the correlative grounds, and also, they establish the potencies and imprints to attain these grounds [in the long run]. One may examine if these views could be taken to mean the same thing.

According to the *Vajra Garland* and the *Drop of Mahamudra—the Great Seal,* the fourteen grounds are established as follows: each of the elevan vase empowerments and the three higher empowerments is a ground in itself. These fourteen grounds are correlative to the ground of Aspiring Activity as the first and the thirteen grounds mentioned in the *Unsurpassed Clear Expression.*

It would be absurd if we were to literally take the fourteen empowerments as the fourteen grounds. It would be absurd because we would have to say that as soon as we received the fourteen empowerments of Guhyasamaja we would attain the fourteen grounds simultaneously. This means that as many of us have received the fourteen empowerments many times we would have become Buddhas already. But we are not, are we? However, to say that the fourteen empowerments are not the same as the fourteen grounds does not preclude their being correlated. The *Clear Lamp* says that they are correlated from the view point of certain concomitant factors.

It is stated in many texts that each empowerment establishes a certain latencies or potencies on the mind in order to achieve a particular ground. Elsewhere it is also stated that it is as fortunate to attain the fourteen empowerments as it is to attain the grounds. Our author, Yangchen Galo, advises us to find out whether these two statements mean the same thing.

PRESENTING FIFTEEN AND SIXTEEN GROUNDS:

> The modes of establishing fifteen and sixteen grounds is as follows: If the Aspiring Activity is taken as the first ground, in accordance with the *Drop of Exalted Wisdom* quoted earlier, there are eleven grounds, up to the Cloud of Dharma. The ground of a non-trainee is divided into four—the Omnipresent Light (kun tu 'od), the All-Illuminating Light (kun tu snang wa mched pa'i 'od), the Light of Illuminating Attainment (kun tu snang wa thob pa'i 'od) and the Inexpressible and Immeasurable (brjod du med pa tshad med pa). [In addition to the eleven grounds] when these [four] are counted individually there are fifteen grounds. These [latter grounds] are taken as Truth Body, Emanation Body, Enjoyment Body and Body of Great Bliss respectively. Alternatively, if the Very Joyous is taken as the first [ground] and the eleventh ground, Omnipresent Light, is divided into five—Emanation Body, Enjoyment Body, Truth Body, Body of Great Bliss and Wisdom Body—there are fifteen grounds. According to this system suchness (emptiness) characterized by the dual purities is considered as the Truth Body, and wisdom which realizes this Truth Body is regarded as the Wisdom Body.
> The Wisdom Truth Body is called the Wisdom ground

since it is the sixteenth ground when counted from the ground of Aspiring Activity. Acharya Guhyavajra's *Commentary on Difficult Points* (*dka' 'grel*) says: "[They] are correlated to the sixteen [grounds] like the Aspiring Activity." Therefore, according to the intention of the *Drop of Exalted Wisdom* (*ye shes thig le*) the path of a non-trainee is presented as four or five grounds.

Although in the Tantric context the grounds are given either the same or different names as those of the Perfection Vehicle and the list of grounds is longer, this is merely a matter of classification of the grounds of ordinary beings and the grounds of Superiors (Aryas), both trainees and non-trainees. These presentations are not contradictory and either of them is acceptable.

According to many eminent Indian realized masters' (*mkas grub gnyis ldan*) elucidations of the meaning of the Tantras, there is no ground higher than the eleventh—the Omnipresent Light. Therefore, the eleventh ground of the Perfection Vehicle—the Omnipresent Light—and the thirteenth ground of Tantra—the Vajra Holder—should be understood as synonymous.

The mode of establishing the fifteen grounds, according to the *Drop of Exalted Wisdom*, is that if the Aspiring Activity is taken as the first ground, the Cloud of Dharma becomes the eleventh ground. In addition to them the ground of a non-trainee is divided into four individual grounds: Omnipresent Light, All Illuminating Light, Attainment of Ever Brilliant Light and the Inexpressible and Immeasurable. These last four grounds are also called the Truth Body, the Emanation Body, the Complete Enjoyment Body and the Great Bliss Body respectively. Another way of establishing the fifteen grounds is to take the Very Joyous as the first ground and divide the eleventh ground—Omnipresent Light—into five grounds, with the last one being called the Wisdom Body. According to this list suchness or emptiness, which is characterized by the dual purities, is considered as the Truth Body. The dual purities are the primordial natural purity (*rang bzhin rnam dag*) and the purity of adventitious defilements (*glo bur rnam dag*). In other words, the emptiness of the omniscient mind is primordially pure in its nature and it is also pure of all the adventitious defilements. Therefore, it is the Natural Truth Body. The omniscient mind itself is taken as the Wisdom

Truth Body; its experience of the great bliss is known as the Great Bliss Body.

The mode of establishing the sixteen grounds is to add the ground of Aspiring Activity, as the first, to the fifteen grounds just mentioned. In this case the Wisdom Truth Body becomes the sixteenth ground. We find a source for this in Acharya Guhyavajra's work, *Commentary on the Difficult Points* (dka' 'grel). The difference between the fifteen and the sixteen grounds arrangements is just a matter of classification and thus, the two listings do not contradict each other. The *Drop of Exalted Wisdom* says that the ground of a non-trainee can be either divided into four or five.

According to many eminent realized Indian scholars there is no ground higher than the eleventh. This means the Omnipresent Light of the Perfection Vehicle and Vajra Holder, the thirteenth ground, of the Tantric Vehicle are synonymous.

TEN GROUNDS CORRELATE THE TWO STAGES:

The way in which the ten grounds, as already explained, correlate the two stages [of Highest Yoga Tantra] in terms of substitute/equivalences (dod thub): According to the intention of the Arya Father [Nagarjuna] and his [spiritual] sons, the generation stage that is meditated upon in order to ripen the mind-stream is correlated to the seventh ground and below, but the way it correlates to each of the seven grounds is not explained. The completion of the coarse and the subtle [levels of the] generation stage, after the mind stream has been already ripened, is correlated to the fresh attainment of the eight ground. But the isolated body and the isolated speech of the completion stage are correlated to the latter part of the eight ground and the ninth ground. The isolated mind and the illusory body are both correlated to the earlier part of the tenth ground, and the clear light and the union of a trainee are both correlated to the latter part of the tenth ground. It is the intention of the *Compendium of Deeds* to correlate the state of union of a non-trainee to the eleventh ground, the Omnipresent Light.

According to Arya Nagarjuna and his spiritual sons, meditation on the generation stage for ripening the mindstream is correlated to the seventh ground and below. But there is no futher explanation of how it corresponds or correlates to each of the grounds up to the seventh. And the mindstream which has been ripened by the completion of the coarse and the subtle levels of the generation stage is correlated to the fresh attainment of the eighth ground. The isolated body and the isolated speech of the completion stage are correlated to the latter part of the eighth and the ninth grounds, whereas the isolated mind and the impure illusory body are correlated to the earlier part of the tenth ground. But the clear light and the state of union of a trainee are correlated to the latter part of the tenth ground. The state of union of a non-trainee is correlated to the eleventh ground of Omnipresent Light.

How do the Ten Grounds Correlate the Two Stages?:

> Although the grounds and paths of Highest Yoga Tantra, such as the generation stage, the three isolations, the illusory body and so forth, and those of the Perfection Vehicle are not literally identical, nonetheless, in terms of [certain] concomitant features, they are considered to be equivalent substitutes for each other. The reason why the completion of the coarse and subtle [levels] of the generation stage, after the mindstream has already been ripend, is correlated to the eight ground is because the accomplishment of the Training in the Purification of the [Buddha] Environment (zhing dad sbyor wa) on the eighth ground of the Perfection Vehicle and the completion of the generation stage are equal in terms of the attainment of an ability to accomplish a special [Buddha] Environment in which one will become a Buddha. The reason for correlating the isolated body and the isolated speech to the ninth ground is that the attainment of the wisdom of purified speech to teach the Doctrine on the ninth ground of the Perfection Vehicle is equivalent to the attainment of control over the wind [breath], the root of speech, on the level of the isolated speech.

Although the generation stage and the various levels of the completion stage—the three isolations, the illusory body, the clear light, and the states of union—and the grounds of the Perfection Vehicle are not identical, they are correlated to each other in terms of certain concomitant factors. The completion of the coarse and the subtle levels of the generation stage is equivalent to the eighth ground in that just as on the eighth ground Bodhisattvas have accomplished what is called the

'Practice for the Pure Environment of One's (Future) Enlightenment' (zhing dag sbyor wa), Tantric meditators who have completed the coarse and subtle levels of the generation stage have also developed the potencies to accomplish the pure environment of their future enlightenment. In his *Ornament for Clear Realization (mngon rtogs rgyan)* Maitreya set forth Bodhisattvas' qualities on the eighth ground in two sets of four qualities each which include their ability to accomplish 'the Pure Environment of One's (Future) Enlightenment' in which they will become Buddhas. As stated earlier, they have accomplished the 'Practice for the Pure Environment of One's (Future) Enlightenment'.

Likewise, there is a reason why the isolated body and the isolated speech are correlated to the latter part of the eighth and the ninth grounds. On the ninth ground of the Perfection Vehicle Bodhisattvas attain the wisdom of pure speech for teaching Dharma since they have attained the 'four analytical wisdoms' (sor rtogs ye she) such as the analytical wisdom of words (i.e. knowing every word of a language, for instance of devas or gods, distinctly) and the analytical wisdom to penetrate the profound meanings of words. Similarly, on the occasion of the isolated speech Tantric meditators have gained control over the breath which is the source of their speech. On this level ordinary speech, which is the basis of isolation and normally considered as being different from mantra, has been realized as being one with mantra. This factor and the wisdom of pure speech of the Perfection Vehicle are concommitant with each other.

> The reason why the isolated mind is correlated to the tenth ground is because the attainment of like-control over mind (sems dbang rjes mthun pa) on the tenth ground of the Perfection Vehicle is equivalent to the mental control of the isolated mind. Similarly, the reason why the illusory body is correlated to the tenth ground is because on the tenth ground of the Perfection Vehicle one receives the great light empowerment from Buddhas which is equivalent to an illusory body's receiving an empowerment from Buddhas. And the reason why the clear light and the union of a trainee are correlated to the latter part of the tenth ground is that the latter part of the tenth ground of the Perfection Vehicle, associated with the extensive factor of method, is increasingly powerful in abandoning the obstructions to knowledge and also because there is no need [for one on the tenth

ground] to train newly in any other path. Similarly, the meaning clear light of the fourth level, associated with an extensive factor of method, is the most powerful for eliminating the obstructions to knowledge and also because on the occassion of the state of union of a trainee there is no need to train newly in any other path. Nevertheless, those of the Perfection Vehicle who are in their final lives [for attaining Enlightenment] must [eventually] enter these paths of the clear light and the state of union.

The isolated mind and the impure illusory body are correlated to the earlier part the tenth ground because on the tenth ground of the Perfection Vehicle, Bodhisattvas have gained similitudes of the ten exclusive powers of a Buddha such as the control over their mind. Like them, those who attained the isolated mind have also gained similitudes of the ten powers. Also, according to the Perfection Vehicle, Bodhisattvas on the tenth ground receive the empowerment of great light from Buddhas, exhorting them to rise up from the meditative equipoise and work for enlightenment. Similarly, Tantric practitioners who have the impure illusory body also receive the third empowerment from Buddhas at midnight and then work for the state of Vajradhara. These two factors also correlate with each other.

The meaning clear light of the fourth level and state of union of a trainee are correlated to the latter part of the tenth ground since Bodhisattvas' on the latter part of the tenth ground of the Perfection Vehicle have integrated fully their meditative equipoise on emptiness with the merits of the three countless aeons. Therefore, their wisdom serves as the direct antidote to the small of the small object of abandonment of the path of meditation; in other words, the final antidote to the last obstruction to omniscient knowledge. This factor is concomitant with the meaning clear light conjoined with the pure illusory body, a vast factor of skillfull method. Due to this method the meaning clear light has become the most powerful antidote for eliminating the last obstruction to omniscient knowledge. Also, according to the Perfection Vehicle, Bodhisattvas on the latter part of the tenth ground have only to familiarize themselves with the path that has already been generated since there is no new path for them to cultivate. Likewise, yogis (Tantric practitioners) in the state of union of a trainee have to only familiarize themselves with the path they have already cultivated for them also there is no new path to be cultivated. But, according to Highest Yoga

Tantra Bodhisattvas of the Perfection Vehicle who are in their final lives must enter the paths of the meaning clear light and the states of union to attain supreme enlightenment.

PRESENTING THE TWO STAGES IN THE FIVE PATHS:

> The mode of presenting the two stages [of Highest Yoga Tantra] in the five paths from the point of view of their entities is as follows:
>
> After having trained one's mindstream by the common paths, the altruistic mind of enlightenment is generated in connection with Highest Mantra. All the paths from then onwards, until one achieves a realization of the completion stage are exclusive paths of the [path of] accumulation of the Highest Tantra. The path of preparation of the Highest Tantra consists of all the paths from such a realization of the completion stage up to the attainment of the meaning clear light of the fourth level. But the meaning clear light of the fourth level is both the path of seeing of the Highest [Tantra] and its first ground. The path of meditation of the Highest Tantra consists of all the paths from the union of a trainee up to the attainment of the union of a non-trainee. Within this [ground] is presented the remaining nine grounds. The union of a non-trainee is the path of no-more learning of the Highest Tantra—[that corresponds to] the Omnipresent Light, described as the eleventh ground in the Perfection Vehicle— and also, the ground of a Vajra-Holder, presented as the thirteenth ground in the [Highest] Tantra.

From the point of view of their nature the two stages of Highest Yoga Tantra are divided into five paths. It is necessary for one to cultivate common paths, such as the 'three principal paths', in order to engage in any of the paths of any Highest Yoga Tantra. As for the paths of Highest Yoga Tantra, its path of accumulation extends from the generation of the altruistic mind of enlightenment (within the context of Highest Yoga Tantra) until the attainment of a realization of the completion stage. The path of preparation of Highest Yoga Tantra extends from the attainment of a realization of the completion stage until the attainment of the meaning clear light of the fourth level. The meaning clear light of the fourth level is the path of seeing and the first ground of Highest Yoga Tantra. According to the Perfection Vehicle, from the entry into a vehicle until one reaches the path of seeing one only ascertains the four noble truths by way of their generic images but on the path of seeing one sees emptiness directly. This is also the case with the meaning clear light of the fourth level of the completion stage. The path of meditation of Highest Yoga Tantra extends from the state of union of a trainee until the attainment of the state of union of a non-trainee. It consists of the remaining nine grounds. The Perfection Vehicle also classifies the path of meditation into nine grounds, such as the small, the middling and the great; each of them is further divided into three, such as the small of the small, the middling of the small and the great of the small. These levels individually constitute a specific antidote to a specific obstruction to knowledge. Each level has 'its own share of an object of abandonment' (rang gi ngo skal gyi spang bya). And each level has two facets: the uninterrupted facet and the liberated facet.

The state of union of a non-trainee is the path of no-more learning of Highest Yoga Tantra; it is also the eleventh ground—Omnipresent Light—of the Perfection Vehicle and the thirteenth ground of the Tantric Vehicle which is called the Vajra Holder.

> In short, the whole of the generation stage constitutes the path of accumulation and the completion stage is divided into three—the paths of preparation, seeing and meditation.

Conclusively speaking, the entire generation stage is the path of accumulation of Highest Yoga Tantra and the completion stage is classified into the remaining paths of preparation, seeing and meditation. The Generation stage also has certain levels but they are included within the 'three types of meditative stabilizations' (ting nge 'zin gsum). They are: the preliminary meditative stabilization (dang po sbyor wa'i ting nge 'dzin), the meditative stabilization of the supreme conqueror of the mandala (dkyil 'khor rgyal mchog gi ting nge 'dzin) and the meditative stabilization of the supreme activities of the conqueror (las rgyal mchog gi ting nge 'dzin).

1. The preliminary meditative stabilization is so called because it is the emanator of the deities of mandala or in other words, it combines method and wisdom inseparably prior to emanating the deities of the mandala.

    This meditative stabilization begins with the *Liturgy of Guhyasamaja* and extends up to the point of 'Consorting with the Knowledge-Woman' ('rig ma 'du byed pa').

2. The meditative stabilization of the supreme conqueror of the mandala is so called because it is the complete setting of the mandalas from having emanated completely the deities of the mandala, from the (seminal) mind of enlightenment of the principal deity and the consort, to setting them in their respective abodes. This meditative stabilization begins with 'Consorting with the Knowledge-Woman,' during which both the resident and the residence mandalas are generated in the lotus organ of the consort and are later withdrawn individually from her lotus and sent forth from one's heart. After performing the general and specific altruistic deeds benefiting sentient beings they are set on their respective seats in the external mandala. This extends up to the point where meditation on the subtle generation stage starts.

3. The meditative stabilization of the supreme activities of the mandala is so called because, from the subtle drop to accomplishing innumerable activities, it mainly sees them to accord with the activities of a Buddha's body, speech and mind. These are all according to the tradition of Arya Nagarjuna.

As mentioned earlier, various levels of the completion stage constitute the three remaining paths. Of them, on the path of preparation yogis ascertain emptiness by way of its generic image; on the path of seeing they ascertain emptiness directly and on the path of meditation they cultivate more and more intimacy with their direct ascertainment of emptiness until they attain supreme enlightenment.

THE TWO OBJECTS OF ABONDONEMENT IN TANTRA:

> In the context of Tantra, the two principal objects to be abandoned are ordinary appearance and ordinary clinging. Of these two, ordinary clinging is explained as the afflictive obstruction to liberation and ordinary appearance is explained as the obstruction to [omniscient] knowledge. As for the ways in which these obstructions are abandoned, according to the assertion of the texts of the Lower Tantric College,, just as the obstructions to liberation are abandoned simultaneously by the meaning clear light of the fourth level, the obstructions to knowledge are also abandoned simultaneously by the meaning clear light of the final trainee.

According to the Perfection Vehicle, the two main obstacles blocking the path of practitioners are: the obstruction to liberation and the obstruction to omniscient knowledge. All other obstructions that are mentioned, such as the 'obstruction to meditative absorptions' (snyoms 'jug gi sgrib pa), are included within these two main obstacles.

In Tantra the two main obstacles are ordinary appearance and ordinary clinging. Ordinary appearance is the obstruction to omniscient knowledge and the ordinary clinging is the obstruction to liberation. In order to eliminate these two obstructions there are techniques in Tantra for generating oneself in the clear form of a deity, holding divine pride and also seeing the whole environment as the inestimable divine mansion. Such techniques are exclusive to Tantra. The Perfection Vehicle does not have such effective and speedy techniques for eliminating ordinary appearance and ordinary clinging and reaching the supreme enlightenment. We have to be very watchful of those two obstructions, even when we are practising deity yoga. We may generate ourselves as a deity but might still see and cling to ourselves as being ordinary. Of course, I do not mean to say that we are not ordinary persons in general. I am not denying this fact. But what I am saying here is that when through deity yoga we have generated ourselves as a deity from within emptiness we must not think of ourselves as being ordinary or see ourselves as such. Otherwise, our deity yoga does not become an antidote to our ordinary appearance and ordinary clinging which are predominantly prevalent in us. This is the crux of the matter in Tantric practice.

With regard to abandoning the two main obstructions, according to one system they are abandoned simultaneously but according to the other they are abandoned gradually. In the Perfection Vehicle, delusions are classified into primary delusions and secondary delusions. There is in fact a detailed exposition on them in the Perfection Vehicle treatises. It is difficult to say whether or not all such delusions and obstructions are included within the two main obstructions of Tantra. However, as I have told you before, ordinary appearance is asserted as the obstruction to omniscient knowledge and ordinary clinging as the obstruction to liberation. According to the course texts of the Lower Tantric College, just as the meaning clear light of the fourth level abandons all the obstructions to liberation simultaneously, the meaning clear light of the final trainee also abandons all the obstructions to omniscient knowledge simultaneously.

Although, from the point of view of the objects of abandonment, the path of meditation of the state of union of a trainee is not presented as nine grounds; however, for the meaning clear light to be able to abandon the obstructions to knowledge it must be associated with the collection of merit. Such a collection is divided into three—the small, the middling and the great. Each of them is [further] divided into three—the small, the middling and the great. Therefore, it is from this point of view that the path of meditation is presented into nine grounds. But, according Khedrup Je's *Festivity of Engaging in Yogas* (rnal 'jor rol pa' dga' ston), a text of the Upper Tantric College of Central Tibet reveals the symbolized Meaning Vajra, and asserts that the obstructions to knowledge are divided into nine, such as the great, the middling and the small etc., and these are abandoned sequentially by the nine [levels] of the path of meditation of the state of union of a trainee.

These presentations of grounds in the context of Highest [Yoga] Tantra are made from the point of view of the spontaneously generated subjective great bliss perceiving objective emptiness. Every instance of the spontaneously generated great bliss is asserted as a specific ground, as is clearly stated [elsewhere]: "They are all instances of joy (bliss) Intellectually imputed as grounds."

The same source states that it is not from the point of view of the objects of abandonment that the state of union of a trainee is divided into the nine grounds of the path of meditation, but for the meaning clear light to have full power to eliminate obstructions to omniscience it must be supported by the collections of merit from the small to the middle to the great. Each of them is further divided into three—the small, the middle and the great. It is from this point of view that the nine grounds are presented within the path of meditation.

But the course texts of the Upper Tantric College, quote Khedrup Rinpoche who states that the nine levels of the path of meditation of the state of union of a trainee serially abandon the nine sets of obstructions to omniscience from the great of the great object of abandonment to the small of the small object of abandonment. The source which Khedrup Rinpoche quotes in his *Festivity of Engaging in Yoga* (rnal 'byor rol pa'i dga' ston) describes the symbolized vajra. The vajra, as a hand symbol which is placed on one's hand during an empowerment, is the symbolic vajra. The vajra which it symbolizes is the wisdom of inseparable bliss and emptiness. This is the 'definitive' or 'real' vajra. This wisdom has nine levels which are the antidotes for serially abandoning the nine sets of obstructions to omniscience.

All the presentations of grounds in Highest Yoga Tantra are made from the point of view of how the spontaneous great blissfull wisdom ascertains objective emptiness. Each level of such a wisdom is presented as an individual ground. As stated clearly elsewhere, "They are all instances of joy/bliss; Intellectually imputed as grounds."

THE FIVE PATHS:

> Notwithstanding that, just as in the lower Tantras and other vehicles, the realization of suchness (emptiness) arising from mundane meditation is presented as the path of preparation; the new direct realization of suchness as the path of seeing, and cultivating [more and more] intimacy with what has already been realized (i.e. emptiness) as the path of meditation. Moreover, these are presented in terms of the main paths. Otherwise there is no certainty with regard to the other [paths] included in them for ascertaining the meaning of suchness.

The paths of preparation, seeing and meditation are presented in accordance with the Perfection Vehicle and the three lower Tantras. The path of preparation ascertains emptiness by way of its generic image as a result of a mundane or worldly meditation; the path of seeing ascertains emptiness newly and directly and; the path of meditation generates more and more intimacy with the direct ascertainment of emptiness. All these paths ascertain emptiness for they are the main paths. But, there are other paths included in them which do not necessarily ascertain emptiness as they do. For instance, the conventional mind of enlightenment associated with the path of seeing has the same entity as the path of seeing but that it does not ascertain emptiness. By extension we can understand that all the paths included in the two stages of Guhyasamaja do not necessarily have to ascertain emptiness although the main paths do ascertain emptiness.

THE SUPREMACY OF GUHYASAMAJA OVER OTHER TANTRAS:

> As *Khedrup Je's Short Writing* (*mkhas sgrub rje'i yig chung*)
> says, "Moreover,if first one understands Guhyasamaja, one
> would effortlessly [easily] understand others (viz: Tantras).
> But, if the order is reversed then the benefits will be fewer;
> therefore, [I shall] teach Guhyasamaja first." And here the
> glorious Guhyasamaja has been explained according to the
> Arya [Nagarjuna] tradition. The *Bright Lamp* (*sgron gsal*) says,
> "This is the supreme subsidiary practice incorporating the
> meanings of all Tantras." As stated, the meanings of all
> Tantras are incorporated within these five levels of the path
> of Guhyasamaja: taking the generation stage as first, then the
> level of focusing on the mind, the illusory body, the clear
> light and the state of union.

Khedrub Rinpoche's Short Writing says that he taught Guhyasamja
first because if practitioners could comprehend the Guhyasamaja Tantra
then they would easily understand the other Highest Yoga Tantras. But
if the order of presentation is reversed then the benefits would be fewer.
I feel we are doing fine since we are here studying the paths and grounds
of Guhyasamaja according to the noble tradition of Arya Nagarjuna and
his spiritual sons.

With reference to Guhyasamaja, *Bright Lamp* (*sgron gsal*) also says
that it is the supreme complimentary practice (sgrub pa'i yan lag
mchog) which incorporates the meaning of all Tantras under its five
outlines:

1. The generation stage.
2. The level of focussing on the mind (the isolated body and the
   isolated speech).
3. The illusory body.
4. The clear light.
5. The state of union.

OTHER TANTRAS INCORPORATED WITHIN THE FIVE PATHS OF GUHYASAMAJA:

> The ways in which other Tantras are incorporated within the
> five levels of Guhyasamaja are as follows: All the paths of the
> three lower Tantras are incorporated within these five levels
> of Guhyasamaja from the point of view of their functions; the
> six branched-yoga of Kalachakra is incorporated within them

from the point of view of equivalent substitute; and the paths of other Highest [Yoga Tantras] are incorporated within them from the point of view of their entities. Although the generation stages of other Highest [Yoga Tantras] are not exactly the same as this [Guhyasamaja] generation stage, they mean the same thing when understood as ripening the roots of virtue for the thorough generation of the completion stage. Notwithstanding whether or not the terms 'isolated mind', 'illusory body', 'clear light' and 'state of union', which have been explained here [in this text], are actually used in other Highest Yoga Tantras, one has to know how these relate to their [respective] completion stages. [Likewise] yogas such as the yoga of inner heat and the yoga of drop explained in other [Tantras] are incorporated within the isolated speech explained here. All the explanations of penetrating the vital points of other parts of the body prior to penetrating the vital points at the heart are incorporated within the isolated body [explained] here. For these reasons, after ascertaining well the paths of the glorious Guhyasamaja and how the paths of other Highest Yoga Tantras are incorporated within them, one will attain supreme fearless confidence with regard to [elucidating] their meanings. As Manjunath Lama Tsongkhapa says: "Ascertaining it—the path of Guhyasamaja—bestows upon one the supreme fearless confidence with regard to (elucidating] all scriptures."

If asked, "How does Guhyasamaja incorporate the paths of all other Tantras?" It is as follows: All the paths of the three lower Tantras are included in the five levels of Guhyasamaja from their functional point of view. The six subsidiary yogas of the Kalachakra are included in them from the point of view of their correlatives. The six subsidiary yogas[66] are:

1. The Individual withdrawal (sor sdud).
2. The Concentration (bsam gtan).
3. The Retention ('dzin pa).
4. The Subsequent mindfulness (rjes dran).
5. The Vitality and Exertion (srog rtsol).
6. The Meditative stabilization (ting nge 'dzin).

Except for the path of the *Kalachakra Tantra*, the paths of other

Highest Yoga Tantras are included in the two stages of the Guhyasamaja from the point of view of their nature or entity. The generation stages of other Highest Yoga Tantras and that of the Guhyasamaja are not exactly the same, yet if one understands them as ripening the virtues for thoroughly generating the completion stage, they mean the same. With this we can realize that the ultimate purpose of all the generation stages of the Highest Yoga Tantras is the same, i.e. preparing our mind to be ripened by the completion stage. Other Highest Yoga Tantras may or may not use terms, such as 'the isolated mind', and 'the illusory body' but we should know how to correlate them to their completion stages. Also, what is explained in other Tantras, such as 'the Inner Heat Yoga' and 'the Yoga of Drop' are included within the level of the isolated speech of Guhyasamaja. In the Heruka Tantra there is 'the Inner Heat Yoga' of visualizing short 'a' at the navel channel wheel, which allows one to withdraw winds into the central channel; this corresponds to the Vajra Recitation and the Vitality and Exertion of Guhyasamaja Tantra. Therefore, it is included in the isolated speech. Similarly, the yogas of penetrating other vital points of the body before penetrating the vital point at the heart so that the winds could enter, abide and dissolve in the central channel are included in the isolated body of Guhyasamaja. To illustrate this, in Heruka practice one penetrates the twenty-four vital points on the body either by visualizing a deity and his consort in union at each point or generating the channels and elements at each point into deities.

In conclusion our text tells us that, for the reasons just given, if we understand well the path of Guhyasamaja—especially how its various levels include the paths of other Highest Yoga Tantras from the points of view of their nature, function and correlations—we would gain supreme fearless confidence in the meanings of all Tantras as Lama Tsongkhapa has well remarked.

There, we come to the end of this presentation of the paths and grounds of Glorious Guhyasamaja according to the noble tradition of Arya Nagarjuna. The other system of Guhyasamaja, as already stated earlier, is that of the master (Acharya) Jnanapada.

Colophon:

The Vajra vehicle is the peak of all teachings
Its even a rare fortune to hear its beautiful name
This jewel more precious than anything else
Is obtained by the wealth of millions of past [lives'] merits.
Limited is [my] knowledge by learning and by birth
But, this hundred petalled lotus of [my] intelligence
Blossoms in the rays of sunlight
Of the excellent explanation of Manjunath.
[Accumulated on it] is the honey-like essence
Of all the vital points and hence
[It is] an excellent treat for fortunate bees.
Although it is inappropriate for the dull like me
To speak boastfully of the vast and profound topic;
But, at the repeated and persistent requests
Of the faithful, diligent and intelligent one
[I] composed this to benefit others.
By this virtue, in all lifetimes
May [we] never be misled on paths seemingly correct;
Without hindrances, may we accomplish
Hearing, Contemplation and Meditation
Of the sublime integrated path
Of all the Sutras and Tantras.
In compliance with persistent requests from the faithful,
diligent and intelligent Bhikshu Grags pa Chos bzang of
Khe-sha-thu, I, the lazy Yangchen Gawai Lodoe, taking dust
from the feet of many holy realized masters on the crown of
my head, have composed this for myself and also to repay
the kindness of others.

Sarve hidentu.

By the merits of publishing mechanically
This text of the paths and grounds
Of the profound and secret Guhyasamaja,
May we be cared for
By the Compassionate—Avalokiteshvara
Until cyclic existence is emptied
[of sentient beings].

I, the abbot Lobsang Nyima, composed this dedication prayer for the publication of five hundred copies of this text of the paths and grounds of Tantra. His Holiness the Dalai Lama has authorized its inclusion in the educational syllabus for many new students admitted to his personal monastery— Namgyal Datsang—in 1979 and others who will be admitted in the future.

Sarva Mangalam.

May this edition prevail.

A Short Review:

The generation stage of the Guhyasamaja is an antidote to ordinary appearance and ordinary clinging. These are, as I have already explained, the two main obstacles identified in the Tantric system. Ordinary appearance here does not mean simply the ordinary appearance of oneself alone but also the ordinary appearance of everything that exists. Similarly, ordinary clinging also encompasses all types of clinging to the ordinariness of everything. Of these two obstacles, the former is the obstruction to omniscience and the latter is the obstruction to liberation. How does the generation stage act as their antidote? There are different types of antidotes to obstacles along the paths. I shall base my explanation on Khedrup Rinpoche's *An Ocean of Attainments of the Generation Stage (bskyed rim dngos grub rgya mtsho)*. The way in which a transcendental path eliminates its object of abandonment is different from the way a worldly path eliminates its object of abandonment. For example, the actual antidotes to ordinary appearance and ordinary clinging are the meaning clear light of the final trainee and the meaning clear light of the fourth level respectively. These transcendental paths eliminate their objects of abandonment together with their seeds. Having abandoned them one achieves certain factors of cessation. But, unlike them, a worldly path does not have the power to eliminate its object of abandonment together with its seed. It temporarily overcomes it. For instance, one can take rebirth as a celestial being (deva) of the first stage of concentration of the form realm by following certain worldly paths. In meditation one sees the setbacks of a life in the desire realm but sees life on such a stage of the form realm as relatively more pleasant and peaceful. But the attainment of such a rebirth is temporary as one will sooner or later fall from it. The way the generation stage acts as an antidote to ordinary appearance and ordinary clinging is by way of helping practitioners bring about their cessation. In general, everything including ourselves appears to us as being ordinary and we cling to everything as such. In order to stop   ordinary appearance and ordinary clinging the generation stage practice primarily involves generating ourselves as a deity or deities from within emptiness, seeing our environment as an inestimable celestial mansion and holding divine pride. Seeing ourselves as a deity or deities and the environment as an inestimable celestial mansion counteracts ordinary appearance. And holding divine pride counteracts ordinary clinging with regard to them. Of these two, meditating on the divine pride of the resident and residence mandalas, as an antidote to the ordinary pride, is the primary. And secondary to it is meditating on the aspects of the resident and residence mandalas to cease the ordinary appearance. By merely meditating on deity yoga if the ordinary appearance and ordinary clinging of impure environment and inhabitants within, for the mental consciousness, are transformed into a very pure divine appearance and a strong divine pride which spontaneously and effortlessly last for a very long time, this in essence is the meaning of the cessation of ordinary appearance and clinging by the generation stage.

When experienced meditators of deity yoga stay in a meditative state of the generation stage, their sensory consciousnesses also cease to receive ordinary appearances. This, however, is not the purpose of meditating on the generation stage. The reason why sensory consciousnesses do not receive ordinary appearances of their objects is because they are lacking the 'immediately preceding condition' (de ma thag rkyen) of a mental consciousness. It is necessary for every consciousness to have three conditions for its arisal and functioning. The three conditions are: the fundamental condition of a sensory faculty (bdag rkyen), an objective condition (dmigs rkyen) and the immediately preceding condition (de ma thag rkyen) of the mental consciousness. If any of them is missing a perception can not take place. For the same reason, when we practise deity yoga with concentration, even if our eyes are kept open we can not perceive ordinary appearances although the objects are before our eyes. This is so because the immediately preceding condition for the senses to see things as ordinary is lacking. Acharya Dharmakirti says when one's mind is absorbed in to an object, it would be powerless to perceive any other object. However, as soon as we divert our attention from a particular object the immediately preceding condition arises, so do the sensory perceptions of other appearances. Though I have explained this to you before, once again I would like to emphatically state that while practising the generation stage, at all time it is of paramount importance to generate strong ascertainment of how the aspects of mandala and everything that appear to our mind do not exist the way they appear to exist to our ordinary perception and train ourselves to reflect on them like an illusion. And also train ourselves to see that all of them is a play of the non-dual bliss and emptiness. Meditating single pointedly on the generation stage we are able to cut off ordinary appearance and ordinary clinging but these arise as we stop meditating. Later, when we reach the meaning clear light of the fourth level, ordinary clinging will not arise even in the post-meditational period. Similarly, when we reach the meaning clear light of the final trainee ordinary appearance will never arise for us.

I would like to restate here that cultivating the altruistic mind of enlightenment is a must in order to practise Tantra which is the peak of Greater Vehicle. Else, just as the attachment to this life prevents us from working for future lives, seeking one's own happiness and solitary peace alone prevents us from striving for enlightenment to bring about the complete welfare of all sentient beings.

Question: From what level does a practitioner who has completed the paths of the Perfection Vehicle enter the path of Highest Yoga Tantra?

Answer: Such a practitioner enters the path of Highest Yoga Tantra from the level of the meaning clear light. This means completing the paths of the Perfection Vehicle is equivalent to the levels of three isolations which he or she can skip.

Question: Can anyone enter the Tantric Vehicle afresh?

Answer: Yes, but he or she should at first practise common paths, such as the three principal paths and then enter the Tantric path. The three principal paths are: renunciation or the determined wish to be liberated, the altruistic mind of enlightenment and the wisdom which ascertains emptiness. It would be best if one has genuinely generated the three principal paths in one's mindstream before engaging in Tantric practice. Even if one does not have them genuinely present in one's mind at least one should have strong enthusiasm for them and cultivate them as much as possible. Most of us do not have the three principal paths genuinely present in our minds but we do practise Tantra, don't we? The necessity for generating them in order to practise Tantra is emphasized by a lama during an empowerment. His Holiness the Dalai Lama emphatically tells us to at least contrive the three principal paths during his empowerments. Also, it is essential that we should see our teacher in the form of a deity, especially when we receive empowerment from him. The teachings we receive on such themes implant the seeds in us to experience them genuinely in the near future. We should do our best to germinate these seeds into actual realizations.

Question: Could you explain further the four kayas or bodies of a Buddha?

Answer: There are four kayas or bodies of a Buddha. They are: The Complete Enjoyment Body, the Emanation Body, The Natural Truth Body and the Wisdom Truth Body. These bodies literally exist on the ground of a Buddha. In order for anyone to actualize them by following a tantric path, it is essential at first to receive an appropriate empowerment. This is because 'empowerment' is the door to enter the tantric path. Those who want to practise Guhyasamaja must first receive a Guhyasamaja empowerment. The vase empowerments purify the defilements of the body and empower one to practise the generation stage. Generation stage practice involves meditating on both the resident and residence mandalas which act as a substantial cause for actualizing those mandalas literally existing on the ground of a Buddha.

As for the Complete Enjoyment Body it is characterized by the thirty two noble signs and the eighty auspicious signs. It also literally exists on the ground of a Buddha. Its attainment must be preceded by the attainment of the pure illusory body characterized by those remarkable signs. The attainment of the pure illusory body must be preceded by the attainment of the impure illusory body with the similitudes of the signs. Its attainment must be preceded by the attainment of the three isolations, which is preceded by the yogas of the generation stage. On the generation stage one arises in the form of the primordial protector, the Complete Enjoyment Body. For this, one must receive the secret empowerment that implants the seed of such an enlightened body in one's mind and empowers one to practise the completion stage. This enlightened body is the source of the Emanation Body which can directly work for ordinary people like us.

The Truth Body, which is divided into two as mentioned before, also literally exists on the ground of a Buddha and it always remains firmly within the sphere of emptiness. For the sake of attaining this body one must actualize the spontaneous blissful meaning clear light of the fourth level which ascertains emptiness directly. But this realization must be preceded by a series of realizations such as the conceptual ascertainment of emptiness through its generic image and taking the three resultant enlightened bodies as the paths. One must receive the wisdom-knowledge empowerment that implants the seed for actualizing such a body and empowers one to meditate on the ultimate clear light.

Similarly, the state of union of Vajradhara characterized by the seven features exists on the ground of a Buddha. It's attainment must be preceded by the attainment of the state of union of a trainee. For this one must receive the word empowerment concerning the clear light and the states of union. Such an empowerment purifies one's collective defilements of body, speech and mind, implants the seeds of the states of union in one's mind and empowers one to meditate on the states of union. These are the substantial causes for achieving the four bodies of a Buddha. For us to achieve them, the order of practice is that we should first listen to the teachings on the three principal paths and then practise them. And then we should receive an empowerment of Highest Yoga Tantra and engage in practices ranging from the generation stage to the completion stage by following the instructions of a qualified lama or master. With the right understanding and the right practice we will certainly reach supreme enlightenment. Lord Vajradhara himself said that should a practitioner practise the instructions in an orderly way he or she would certainly attain enlightenment either in this or in successive lives.

Part Five
Appendices:

2. The Mode of Progression on the Completion Stage:

   a. Its Definition

   b. Its Divisions

      i. . Isolated Body

      ii. Isolated Speech

      iii. Isolated Mind

      iv. Illusory Body

      v. Clear Light

      vi. State Of Union

   c. Its Etymological Explanation

   d. The Mode of Transference from a Lower Level to a Higher Level

      i. The Mode of Transference from the Level of Isolated Body to the Level of Isolated Speech

      ii. The Mode of Transference from the Level of Isolated Speech to the Level of Isolated Mind

      iii. The Mode of Transference from the Level of Isolated Mind to the Level of an Illusory Body

      iv. The Mode of Transference from the Level of an Illusory Body to the Level of the Meaning Clear Light

      v. The Mode of Transference from the Level of the Meaning Clear to the State of Union.

   e. The Mode of Actualizing Results

II. The Mode of Establishing the Ten Grounds etc., And the Five Paths

   A. How Tantras and Commentarial Treatises Present Them

   B. Presentation of a Summary

BIBLIOGRAPHY:

1. Sutras and Tantras

Wisdom Gone Beyond Sutras
  Prajnana-paramita-sutras
  Sher phyin gyi mdo
  Translators:
  P....., Vol...
Chakrasamvara Root Tantra
  Shri Chakrasambaraguhya-acinta-tantraraja
  Dpal 'khor lo sdom pa'i gsang wa bsam gyis mi khyab pa'i rgyud
  kyi rgyal po
  Translators: Gayadhara and Shakya Yeshes
  P30, Vol. 3
Compendium of the Wisdom Vajra
  Vajrajnana-samuccaya-nama-tantra
  Ye shes rdo rje kun las bstud pa
  Translators: Jnanakara, Khu ston dngos grub and Rev. Tshul khrims
  rgyal wa
  P84, Vol. 3
Drop of Mahamudra the Great Seal
  Shri Mahamudra-tilakam-nama-yogini-tantraraja-adhipati
  Dpal phyag rgya chen po'i thig le zhes bya wa rnal 'byor ma chen
  mo'i rgyud kyi rgyal po'i mnga' bdag
  Translators: Chos kyi ye shes, dpal shes rab gsang wa and phyug
  'tshams dgra bcom
  P12, Vol. 1-2
Drop of Exalted Wisdom
  Shri Jnantilaka-yogini-tantraraja-paramamahadbhutam-nama
  Dpal ye shes thig le rnal 'byor ma'i rgyud kyi rgyal po mchog tu
  rmad tu 'byung wa zhes bya wa
  Translator: Shri Prajnagupta
  P14, Vol. 2
Explanatory Tantra Vajra Garland
  Shri Vajramala-abhidhana-mahayogatantra-sarvatantrahridaya-

rahasya-vibhanga-iti

Rnal 'byor chen po'i rgyud rdo rje phreng wa mngon par brjod pa rgyud thams cad kyi snying po gsang wa rnam par phye wa zhes bya wa

Translators: Sujanashrijnana and Zhi wa'i 'od

P82, Vol. 3

Guhyasamaja Root Tantra

Sarvatathagata-kaya-vak-citta-rahasyo guhyasamaja-nama-mahakalparaja

De bzhin gshegs pa thams cad kyi sky gsung thugs kyi

gsang chen gsang wa 'dus pa zhes bya wa brtag pa'i rgyal po chen po

Translators: Shraddhakaravarman, Rin chen bzang po, Rev. Rje btsun nyi ma'i dbang po and Chos rje dpal

P81, Vol. 3

Hevajra Tantra

Hevajra-tantra-raja-nama

Kyehi rdo rje zhes bya wa rgyud kyi rgyal po

Translator: Gayadhara, Sakya ye shes, Rev. Gzhon nu dpal

P10, Vol. 1

Ornament of Vajra Essence Tantra

Shri Vajrahrdayalamkara-tantra-nama

Dpal rdo rje snying po rgyan gyi rgyud ces bya ba

Translators: Kamalagupta and Mnga' bdag lha ye shes rgyal mtshan

P86, Vol. 3

Prophetic Revelation of Thought (Explanatory Tantra)

Sandhivyakarana-nama-tantra

Dgons pa lung bstan pa zhes bya wa'i rgyud

Translators: Dharmashribhadra and Rin chen bzang po

P83, Vol. 3

Samputa Tantra

Samputi-nama-mahatantra

Yang dag par sbyor wa zhes bya wa'i rgyud chen po

Translators: Gayadhara and Shakya Yeshes

P26, Vol. 2-3

The Subsequent Tantra of Guhyasamaja

Uttaratantra?

'dus pa'i rgyud phyi ma

Translators:

P.?..Vol. ?

Unsurpassed Clear Expression
  Abhidhana-uttaratantra-nama
  Mngon par brjod pa'i rgyud bla ma zhes bya wa
  Translators: Dipankarashrijnana, Rin chen bzang po, Rev. Jnanashri,
  Chos kyi brtson 'grus and Ananda etc.
  P17, Vol. 2

2. Indian Masters' Treatises

Aryadeva
  Compendium of Deeds
  Carya-melapaka-pradipa
  Spyod pa bsdus pa'i sgron ma
  Translators: Shraddhakaravarman and Rin chen bzang po
  P2668, Vol. 61
Buddhashrijnanapada
  Drop of Liberation
  Mukti-tilaka-nama
  Grol wa'i thig le zhes bya
  Translators: Kamalaguhya and Ye shes rgyal mtshan
  P2722, Vol. 65
Chandrakirti
  Bright Lamp
  Pradipoddyotana-nama-tika
  Sgron ma gsal war byed pa zhes bya wa'i rgya cher bshad pa
  Translators: Shraddhakaravarman, Rin chen bzang po,
    Shrijnanakara, Lhas bstas and Rev. Nag po
  P2650, Vol. 59-60
Jnanaparama
  Commentary of the Drop of Exalted Wisdom
  Shri Jnanatilaka-panjika-guhya-tattva-nama (?)
  Ye shes thig le'i dka' 'grel gsang ba'i de kho na nyid ces bya ba
  Translator: Byang chub 'byung gnas
  P2333, Vol. 55-56
Maitreya
  Ornament for Clear Realization
  Abhi-samayalam-kara
  Mngon par rtogs pa'i rgyan
  Translator:
  P5184, Vol. 88

Nagarjuna
>   *The Five Levels*
>   Panca-krama
>   Rim pa lnga pa
>   Translators: Shraddhakravarman, Rin chen bzang po and Rev. Kamalagupta
>   P2667, Vol. 61
>   *Combined with Sutra*
>   Shri guhyasamaja-mahayogatanttropattikrama-sadhana-sutra-melapaka-nama
>   Rnal 'byor chen po'i rgyud dpal gsang ba 'dus pa'i bskyed pahi rim pa'i bsgom pahi thabs mdo dang bsres pa zhes bya ba
>   Translators: Dharmashribhadra and Rin chen bzang po
>   P2662, Vol. 60-61

Nagabuddhi Klu'i blo
>   *Graded Presentation* (of Guhyasamaja)
>   Samaja-sadhana-vyavasthana-nama
>   'dus pa'i sgrub thabs rnam par bzhag pa'i rim pa zhes bya wa
>   Translators: ?
>   P2674, Vol. 61-62

Shri Abhayakaraguptapada
>   *Cluster of Quintessential Instructions*
>   Upadesha-manjari-nama-sarvatantrotpannopapanna-samanya-bhashaya
>   Man ngag gi snye ma zhes bya ba rgyud thams cad kyi skyed rzogs thun mong du bstan pa
>   Translators: Shri Ratnarakshitapada and Grub pa dpal bzang po
>   P5024, Vol. 87

Shri Nagarjuna (Dpal klu sgrub)
>   *Commentary on Guhyasamaja Tantra*
>   Shri Guhyasamaja-tantrasya tantratika-nama
>   Dpal gsang ba 'dus pa'i rgyud kyi rgyud 'grel pa zhes bya ba
>   Translator: Mantrakalasha
>   P2648, Vol. 59, 218-3-4, le'u drug pa (chapter) 6

3. Tibetan Masters' Treatises

Gyatsab Chosje (alias Gyaltsab Dharma Rinchen or Gyaltsab Rinpoche)
Ornament of the Essence - A Thorough Commentary of the Wisdom Gone Beyond
Shes rab kyi pha rol tu phyin pa'i man ngag gi bstan bcos mngon par brtogs pa'i rgyan gyi 'grel pa don gsal ba'i rnam bshad snying po'i rgyan
Collected Works (gsung 'bum),TCPP, Vol. Kha
Gyaltsab Je's Notes on the Five Levels
Rgyal tshab rje'i rim lnga'i dzin bris (Rdzogs rim dpyid kyi thig le'i dzin bris?)
Collected Works, TCPP, Vol. Ka.
Khedrup Je (alias Khedrup Gelek Palzang or Khedrup Rinpoche)
General Exposition of Tantras
Rgyud sde spyi'i rnam gzhag
Collected Works (gsung 'bum),TCPP, Vol. Nya
Notes of Khedrup Je's Speech
Mkhas grub rje'i gsung dzin bris (Identified as (Rgyud kyi rgyal po) dpal gsang wa 'dus pa'i rdzogs rim gyi man ngag: *Pith Instruction on the Completion Stage of the Glorious Guhyasamaja, (the king of Tantras)*)
Collected Works, TCPP, Vol. A, pp 812-813.
Khedrup Je's Notes on the Five Levels
Mkhas grub je'i rim lnga'i dzin bris (Identified as (Rgyud kyi rgyal po) dpal gsang wa 'dus pa'i rdzogs rim gyi man ngag: *Pith Instruction on the Completion Stage of the Glorious Guhyasamaja, (the king of Tantras)*)
Collected Works,TCPP, Vol. A, p 828.
Khedrup Je's Short Writing
Mkhas grub je'i yig chung (Identified as (Mkhas grub thams cad mkhyen pa'i man ngag yig chung bzhugs so: *Short Writing of the Pith Instructions of Khedrup Thamcad Khyenpa*)
Collected Works,TCPP, Vol. A. p 860.
Festivity of Engaging in Yogas
Rnal 'jor rol pa'i dga' ston
Collected Works,TCPP, Vol. Ta. p 860-985
Tsongkhapa (alias Je Rinpoche or Gyalwa Lobsang Drakpa or 'jam mgon rgyal wa tsong kha pa chen po)
Commentary on the Levels of the Perfect Realization

Man ngag mthar thug gi mngon par byang chub pa'i rim pa'i bshad pa
Collected Works (gsung 'bum),TCPP, Vol. Cha
A Clear Lamp Illuminating the Five Levels
Dpal gsang wa 'dus pa'i man ngag rim lnga gsal sgron
Collected Works,TCPP, Vol. Ja
Great Exposition of the Stages of Secret Mantra
Rgyal khyab bdag rdo rje 'chang chen po'i lam gyi rim pa gsang wa kungyi gnad rnam par phye wa (Sngag rim chen mo)
Collected Works,TCPP, Vol. Ga
Thorough Illumination of the Meaning of the Principles of Empowerment
Dpal gsang wa 'dus pa mi bskyod rdo rje'i dkyil 'khor gyi cho ga dbang gi don de nyid rab tu gsal wa
Collected Works,TCPP, Vol. Ca
Commentary of the Graded Presentation (of Guhyasamaja)
Rnam gzhag rim pa'i rnam bshad dpal gsang wa 'dus pa'i gnad don gsal wa
Collected Works,TCPP, Vol. Cha
Precious Sprout of Fine Analysis
Rgyud kyi rgyal po dpal gsang wa 'dus pa'i rgya cher bshad pa sgron ma gsal wa'i dkah wa'i gnas kyi mtha' gcod rim po che'i myu gu
Collected Works,TCPP, Vol. Ca
Elucidation of All Hidden Meanings (of Abridged Chakrasámvaratantra)
'khor lo sdom pa bde mchog bsdus rgyud kyi rgya cher bshad pa sbas don kun gsal
Collected Works,TCPP. Vol. Nya

NOTE

The titles of the Sutras and Tantras have been listed according to their English alphabetical order but the treatises of Indian and Tibetan masters have been arranged according to the alphabetical order of their names begining with the Indian masters. The English titles of Sutras, Tantras and treatises are mostly short because of their being the translations of the abbreviated Tibetan titles. However, the complete titles are given in full both in Sanskrit and Tibetan for easy sorting in bibliography.

"P" refers to the Peking Edition of the Tibetan Tripitaka (Tokyo-

Kyoto: Tibetan Tripitaka Research Foundation, 1956) And "TCPP" refers to the Tibetan Cultural Printing Press's catalogue of the Collected Works of the Ominiscient Tsongkhapa and his two (chief) spiritual sons (Rje thams cad mkhyen pa tsong kha pa yab sras gsum gyi gsung 'bum dkar chag bzhugs so) printed in Dharmsala in 1981, the Tibetan Royal Year 2108.

4 Other Related Works

Atisha. *Lamp of the Path to Enlightenment*. Translated by Ven. Losang Norbu Shastri, Central Institute for Higher Tibetan Studies, Sarnath: 1984.

Conzort,Daniel. *Highest Yoga Tantra*. Snow Lion Publications, New York: Ithaca, 1986.

Dhargye, Geshey Ngawang. *Kalachakra Tantra*. Translated by Gelong Jhampa Kalsang (Allen Wallace), Co-ordinating Editor Ivanka Vana Jakic, LTWA, Dharamsala: 1985.

Hopkins, Jeffery. *Emptiness Yoga*. Snow Lion Publications, New York: Ithaca, 1987.

____& Asst. Elizebeth Napper, ed. *Meditation on Emptiness*. Wisdom Publications, London: 1983.

Komito, David Ross. *Nagarjuna's Seventy Stanzas: A Buddhist Psychology of Emptiness*. Translation and commentary by Geshey Sonam Rinchen, Tenzin Dorjee and David Ross Komito. Snow Lion Publications, New York: Ithaca, 1987.

Mulllin, Glenn H. *Death and Dying—The Tibetan Tradition*. ARKANA, London: 1986.

____. *The Practice of Kalachakra*. Snow Lion Publications, New York: Ithaca, 1991.

Napper, Elizebeth. *Dependent Arising and Emptiness*. Wisdom Publications, London: 1989.

Rinpoche, Lati and Jeffery Hopkins. *Death, Intermediate State and Rebirth in Tibetan Buddhism*. Rider and Company, London: 1979.

Shantideva. *A Guide to the Bodhisattva's Way of Life*. Translated by Stephen Batchelor. LTWA, Dharamsala: 1979.

Sherbune, Richard F. *A Study of Atisha's Commentary on Lamp of the Enlightenment Path*. University of Washington, Washington: 1976.

Sopa, Geshe Lhundup, Roger Jackson and John Newman. *The Wheel of*

Time: The Kalachakra in Context. Edited by Beth Simon. Deer Park Books, Madison: 1985.

Thurman, Robert A.F., ed. *The Life and Teachings of Tsongkhapa.* LTWA, Dharamsala: 1982.

Tsongkhapa. *The Yoga of Tibet—The Great Exposition of Secret Mantra 2 and 3.* Edited by Jeffery Hopkins. George Allen and Unwin, London: 1981.

____. *Tantra in Tibet—The Great Exposition of Secret Mantra.* Edited by Jeffery Hopkins. George Allen and Unwin, London: 1977.

Yeshi, Lama. *Introduction to Tantra: A Vision of Totality.* Compiled and edited by Jonathan Landaw, Wisdom Publications, London: 1987.

5 Main Source Treatises

Khedrup Je

An Oceon of Attainments of the Generation Stage of the Glorious Guhyasamaja, the king of all Tantras

Rgyud thams cad kyi rgyal po dpal gsang wa 'dus pa'i bskyed rim dgnos grub rgya mtsho zhes bya wa bzhugs so

Class No Ga-2, 17; Acc No-4085, Tibetan Manuscript Section, LTWA Dharmsala,H.P., India.

Tsongkha pa.

Clear Lamp Illuminating the Five Levels of the Glorious Guhyasamaja, the king of all Tantras

Rgyud kyi rgyal po dpal gsang wa 'dus pa'i man ngag rim pa lnga rab tu gsal wa'i sgron me zhes bya wa bzhugs so

Class No Pa-1, 11; Acc No-2055, Tibetan Manuscript Section, LTWA Dharmsala,H.P., India.

Yangchen Gawai Lodoe

An Eloquent Presentation - A Port of Entry for the Fortunate Ones into the Paths and Grounds of Mantra According to the Glorious Guhyasamaja of the Arya (Nagarjuna) Tradition

Dpal gsang wa 'dus pa 'phags lugs dang mthun pa'i sngags kyi sa lam rnam gzhag legs bshad skal bdzang 'jug ngogs zhes bya wa bzhugs so

Class No Ga-4,34; Acc No-1043, Tibetan Manuscript Section, LTWA, Dharmsala,H.P., India.

NOTES:

1. Sanskrit terms such as 'Mantra' and 'Tantra', which in Tibetan are 'sngags' and 'rgyud' respectively, have been used interchangeably in my translation wherever they have the same meaning in the given contexts.

2. The difference between the Greater and the Lesser vehicles is explained primarily in terms of the scope of the attitude, and all other Buddhist vehicles are included within these two. The Vajra Vehicle, though a part of the Greater Vehicle, is the pinnacle of Buddhism. Symbolically the Vajra stands for indestructibility and skillful means.

3. Tantric Buddhism teaches how to utilize afflictive emotions such as desire and anger in the path. The tremendous energy of these emotions is used skillfully in the path to eliminate themselves, just as poison is used in medicine to detoxify a patient. Deity-yoga is the key practice in Tantra, counteracting ordinary appearances and ordinary clinging, and empowering initiated practitioners to utilize their afflictive emotions in the path to enlightenment.

4. Both the Father and Mother Tantras contain non-dual method and wisdom. However, their emphasis is different. The former emphasizes more the bliss and illusory body which are "the method", while the latter emphasizes more "the wisdom" of clear light.

5. A complete empowerment or initiation (abhishekha) from a qualified master is an essential rite for introducing practitioners to a deity or a host of deities along with their celestial environment, and also empowering them to study and hear commentaries on the concerned Tantra and to cultivate the path to ripen their mindstreams and accomplish the results. It is clearly stated in Tantras such as the *Drop of Mahamudra the Great Seal (phyag chen thig le)* and the *Vajra Garland (rgyud rdo rje 'phreng wa)* that without empowerment there would be no attainments whatsoever. If a master teaches Tantra to a disciple without empowerment and the disciple practices it, even with good understanding, both will fall into great hell. See Khedrup Rinpoche's *An Ocean of All Attainments (bskyed rim dngos grub rgya mtsho)*, pp 14-18.

6. See: *The Three Principle Paths* by Lama Tsongkhapa; refer to Other Related Works in English -1.

7. 'Realization' is deeper than a mere intellectual understanding. Intellectual understanding is more of a head quality but realization is more of a heart quality and, therefore, it is more profound and transforming in its nature.

8. While in cyclic existence the kind of peace and happiness that we seek and experience is not genuine, for it does not last, but changes into or leads to problems and suffering. Of the three types of suffering, this suffering of

change is subtle and hard to realize. Failing to realize this, we cling to the marvels of cyclic existence and thus remain trapped in it.

9. See: *A Guide to the Bodhisattvas' Way of Life* by Bodhisattva Shantideva; refer to Other Related Works in English-5.

10. See: Other Related Works in English -7,8,9 and 10.

11. See 'Introduction'.

12. See *The Life and Teachings of Tsongkhapa*, LTWA; refer to Other Related Works in English -6.

13. Our subtle wind and mind have existed from primordial time and have never been separated from each other. However, they do not normally manifest in us, for our coarse winds and minds function actively and overshadow them.

14. Although this text was not translated from the Sanskrit, a salutation to Guru Vajradhara is made in Sanskrit to plant the seed of this holy language in the mind and also to show that this work is as authoritative as the works translated from the Sanskrit. It is believed that the historical Buddha Shakyamuni revealed the Buddhist Tantras in the form of Guru Vajradhara and hence he is referred to as the Lord of the Sacred and Secret Tantric Teaching.

15. When Manjushri Lama Tsongkhapa comes to our world as the eleventh Buddha in the line of the one thousand Buddhas of this aeon, since he taught and authored authentic commentaries on Tantras, it is reasoned and believed that he will teach Tantra then. And the last Buddha (seng ge'i sgra sgrog) is also believed with reason that he will teach Tantras since he vowed to perform the deeds of all preceding Buddhas including the historical Buddha Shakyamuni who taught Tantra. (Source: Geshe Sonam Rinchen and Geshe Dawa).

16. The lotus mandala is an encoded term which refers to the secret organ of a female consort and the mandala of the ultimate mind of enlightenment refers to the mandala of emptiness.

17. These empowerments from the Vase to the Word must be given in sequence. It would be meaningless to skip the lower empowerments and give the higher ones and recommend that disciples practise the completion stage. (See, Khedrup Rinpoche, opcit, p...).

18. A vajra master is the one who confers empowerment upon a disciple. His or her necessary qualifications, such as holding an unbroken lineage of transmission, a fulfillment of an appropriate retreat and expertise on Tantra are laid down in authentic Tantric sources.

19. See *Kalachakra Initiation, Madison, 1981, Published by Deer Park, Madison, Wisconsin, 1981, pp 74-75*.

20. Ibid., p 76.

21. The *Essence-Ornament (snying po rgyan)* states:'Visualizing well the Vajrasattva adorned with ornaments, bell and vajra as the single body of

all Buddhas (sitting) on the center moon and a white lotus, recite the hundred syllable mantra (yi ge brgya pa) twenty one times in accordance with a standard liturgy. The great realized masters have said that this will seal root transgressions etc. from increasing (flourishing). Hence, practise this in between meditative sessions. But, if it is recited one hundred thousand times one will become completely pure (of the broken vows and commitments). (See, Khedrup Rinpoche, opcit, pp 39-40; the quote in Tibetan is in verses).

22. The two stages of Highest Yoga Tantra purify the three ordinary states - death, the intermediate state and rebirth - which are called the three bases of purification. Purification has different meanings in spirituality but what it means here is: "...Paths which accord with the aspects of the three bases of purification stop these actual states from arising and in place of them give rise to the three (enlightened) bodies of the path and the resultant state which accords with their aspects. This should be understood as the meaning of the two stages, as purifiers, purifying the three bases of purification." (Khedrup Rinpoche, opcit, p 208).

23. Although the path of Highest Yoga Tantra is necessary to attain enlightenment nevertheless the paths of the Perfection Vehicle and the three lower Tantras lead to enlightenment. This is analogous to the lower rungs in a ladder leading to the top, although without the higher rungs they can not do so.

24. '...newly engages in the path....' means a person who may not have practised the path of Highest Yoga Tantra in any previous lives, but enters it for the first time. Such a person can attain enlightenment even in this very lifetime.

25. After dissolving the bodily elements and the deities associated with them "...at the end revitalize the divine pride of oneself as being Vajradhara whose body transforms into a halo of light. This light dissolves from its both ends into the heart in the manner of the evaporation of breath blown on a mirror; feel that one has dissolved into the exalted wisdom of non-dual bliss and emptiness and hold this wisdom as far as mindfulness persists. This is the supreme pith-instruction on the transference of consciousness. It cannot be matched even by most of the highly regarded and high sounding pith-instructions on the transference of consciousness popular in Tibet which could only be afforded by offering gold." (Khedrup Rinpoche, opcit, pp 233-234).

26. See, *Death,Intermediate State and Rebirth* by Lati Rinpoche, translated by Jeffrey Hopkins; refer to Other Related Works-3.

27. It is necessary to guide practitioners on the two stages in sequence according to Highest Yoga Tantras and their commentarial treatises. In terms of the order of meditation, although some earlier Tibetan lamas assert that at the beginning of a session, one can meditate on the generation

stage and then at its end on the completion stage, however, according to Arya Nagarjuna and his spiritual sons one does not meditate on the second stage until the first stage is stabilized. (See, Khedrup Rinpoche, op cit, p-28).

"If asked: what is the extent of the generation stage that must be practised before the completion stage? The twelfth chapter of the *Root Tantra (of Guhyasamaja)* explains the generation stage as meaning the four branches of approximation (bsnyen sgrub yan lag bzhi). The *Bright Lamp* elucidates this to mean (that the generation stage extends) from meditating on the "wisdom ground" (ye shes kyi sa sgom pa) to the end of "supreme activities of the mandala" (las rgyal mchog). Alternatively, a condensed generation stage consists of generating what is known as the four vajras (rdo rje bzhi bskyed). Great Naropa explains that it extends from generating the "wisdom ground" to the "supreme conqueror of the mandala" (dkyil 'khor rgyal mchog) but this is intended to be an extensive generation of the four vajras. The condensed form is from generating the wisdom ground to setting syllables at the vajra and lotus of the father and his consort. This is mentioned explicitly, but one must add to it the subtle (generation stage) and mantra recitation etc. The eleventh chapter of the Bright Lamp explains six single pointed mindfulnesses of the six (Buddha) families from meditating on the wisdom ground to the triple beings and states that engaging in them in four sessions (a day) will ripen one's mind stream. This is the same as the condensed generation stage. There is no mention of a more condensed generation stage than this in the works of Arya Nagarjuna and his spiritual sons. ...Hence, after having ripened one's mind stream by meditating on a complete mandala of the generation stage as explained earlier at least in accordance with the condensed generation stage, one should engage in meditation on the completion stage." (Khedrup Rinpoche, opcit, pp 31-33).

28. "At death on the level of the basis also when the winds dissolve gradually and the four empties dawn, the heart is the final vital point where the winds dissolve. This is so as the *Vajra Garland (rdo rje 'phreng wa)* says: "...Life sustaining wind (srog gi rlung) abides in the heart." When life comes into being, at first the life sustaining wind forms in the heart and it is said that from where it comes into being that it eventually dissolves there." (Khedrup Rinpoche, opcit, p 243).

29. Apart from this description in Buddhist literature of how a mirage takes place I would like to add here my own vivid experience of a mirage seen as water. It was during one of the hot days on the road as we were returning from our West Coast tour to Montana, U.S.A. As our friend Carleen Gonder was driving us from Santa Barbara through Reno Nevada, sitting on the front seat, I saw clearly a mirage at a close range. It truly appeared to be water. This was caused by the sun striking the tar

road. I introduced my friends to "mirage" at the time.

30. "...Therefore, it is stated in the *Actual Levels (sa'i dngos gzhi)* that the place in the mixture of semen and blood where an intermediate being (first) enters is the heart. Subsequently upper and lower parts of the body are formed. Eventually at death consciousness leaves the body from the heart. This accords with Explanatory Tantras of Guhyasamaja and the explanations of the Arya (Nagarjuna) and his spiritual sons." (Khedrup Rinpoche, opcit, p 244).

31. The opening of the seat like 'indestructible drop' means when this drop is no longer able to support the subtlest wind and mind encased within it and they are bound to separate from each other.

32. Even today high lamas and able practitioners in the Tibetan community are often found in the clear light state at death. Though clinically dead, by controlling the process of dying they remain in the clear light state (thugs dam) for a varying number of days as fresh as if they were alive, even in the hottest days in India. This is a fascinating phenomenon to witness. See Glenn H. Mullins' *Death and Dying, The Tibetan Tradition*, ARKANA, London, 1986; refer to Other Related Works-4.

33. See *Death, Intermediate State and Rebirth* by Lati Rinpoche, translated by Jeffrey Hopkins, p 30.

34. In this connection, it is interesting to note that the Tibetans observe the death ceremony for forty nine days, inviting monks to perform rituals and prayers for the deceased person. But after forty nine days he or she will have taken a rebirth - good or bad -according to the precipitating karmic action. A year after his death, the first death anniversary is observed with a grand religious ceremony and a party of some sort, indicating the overcoming of sorrow over his or her death.

35. As for the five stages of foetal development "mer mer po" or the viscous foetus is covered with a membrane as thick as a cream but it is liquid within; inner energy ripens this into "ltar ltar po" or the oval foetus which has become cream-like from within and without, and it is likened to yogurt but has not yet become fleshy; inner energy ripens this into "gor gor po" or the oblong foetus which is fleshy but can not resist pressure; inner energy ripens this into " 'khrang 'gyur" or the hard-fleshy foetus which can resist pressure; inner energy ripens this into "rkang lag 'gyus pa" or the protrusion of bits of these five limbs: two thighs, two shoulders and the head. From then onwards it develops further with hair, nails, body hairs, sense organs such as the eye and the sex organs etc..." (See Khedrup Rinpoche, opcit, pp 270-271).

36. The reason why all the deities of Guhyasamaja have three faces is in order to signify the three aspects of the enlightened body of the ultimate state of union. They are: the conventional illusory body, the ultimate clear light

mind and the indivisibility of the two. (See Khedrup Rinpoche, opcit, p 264).

37. We visualize two Kshitigarbhas at the eyes and two Vajrapanis at the ears but in the list of thirty two deities of Guhyasamaja they are not counted individually but as a pair each. Similarly, we may visualize three hundred and sixty Samantabhadras at the joints of our body, but in the list of thirty two deities of Guhyasamaja, all of them are counted as one. And this is same with the two Rupavajras and two Shabdavajras, counted as one pair each in the list of thirty two deities of Guhyasamaja.

38. It is very important to understand that the 'I' here is not the 'Ego' but the conventional 'I' which exists imputedly and thus, dependently.

39. "...clinging even to emptiness as being truly existent is an incorrigible (distorted) view (gsor mi rung wa'i lta wa)." (Khedrup Rinpoche, opcit, p 97).

40. The four yogas (rnal 'byor bzhi ni) are: yoga (rnal 'byor), subsequent yoga (rjes su rnal 'byor), genuine yoga (shin tu rnal 'byor) and great yoga (rnal 'byor chen po). According to Arya Nagarjuna's *Combined with Sutra (mdor byas)*, from generating the "wisdom ground" to the withdrawing of the "deities of spontaneous imagination" (lhag mos) to the body, are the preliminaries to the actual yoga. The mode of enlightenment through suchness (de bzhin nyid la byang chub pa) and the mode of enlightenment through moon (dzla wa las byang chub pa) are the actual yogas. The remaining three modes of enlightenment (mngon byang lhag ma gsum) are the subsequent yoga (rjes su rnal 'byor). From this to the complete setting of the deities in the body mandala is the genuine yoga (shin tu rnal 'byor). From the blessing of the three doors - body, speech and mind - to the end of the preliminary meditative stabilization is the great yoga (rnal 'byor chen po). According to the Arya's tradition of Guhyasamaja, these four yogas summarize only the preliminary meditative stabilization but not the entire liturgy or Sadhana. (See Khedrup Rinpoche, opcit, p 443).

41. "Meditating on body-mandala (lus dkyil) does not mean simply setting deities at various points of the body. What it means is to take various parts of the body as a basis (individually) for accomplishing the respective deities and meditate on them. Otherwise, the three Lower Tantras too would have mentioned meditating on the body-mandala a number of times. ...As for the body-mandala, without creating them newly, its various parts have been in existence since the time of birth from parents. These are taken as the bases from which the body-mandala is accomplished and for this reason it is called `uncreated mandala (ma bcos pa'i dkyil 'khor'." (Khedrup Rinpoche, opcit, p-307). "...For instance, one's eye sensory faculty transforms into the syllable THILM and one meditates that this transforms into Kshitigarbha...". (Ibid, p-309).

42. Each of our five aggregates etc are generated into deities. For instance, our

form aggregate in the aspect of OM arises as white Vairochana with three faces and six arms. In this regard the syllable OM has the same nature as our form aggregate. You can relate this explanation to the remaining mantra syllables and the associated aggregates etc.

43. The yoga of subtle drop (phra thig gi rnal 'byor) is cultivated on two levels: the level of beginners, and the level after completing the coarse yoga. On the level of beginners although the main focus is on the coarse yoga of the generation stage in four sessions daily, nevertheless, in order to eliminate laxity and excitement the subtle drop yoga is occasionally cultivated. If laxity is strong a subtle symbol is visualized at the tip of one's nose in order to eliminate it and for excitement a subtle drop is visualized at the lower end (of the central psychic channel). On this level one neither visualizes symbols and deities into the subtle drop nor emanates and withdraws them to it. These are done after seeing signs indicating the stability of the mind on the symbol and the drop. After completing the coarse yoga (of the generation stage), the main focus is on the two subtle drops for day and night. The purpose of doing this is to perfect the stability of the mind on its focus. (See Khedrup Rinpoche, opcit, pp 392-393).

44. "As for the seats, there are thirty one variegated lotus seats common (to all the deities) and as for the uncommon seats, there are moon seats for peaceful deities such as Vairochana in the east. Except Mamaki, who has a vajra seat, all other deities in the south have jewel seats, all in the west have red lotus seats and all in the north have crossed vajra seats. In its section on the "supreme conqueror of the mandala" (dkyil 'khor rgyal mchog) the *Condensed Sadhana (sgrub thabs mdor byas)* explicitly and implicitly states that the principal (deity) and the ten fierce ones have sun seats." (Khedrup Rinpoche, opcit, pp 168-169).

45. "Although Arya Nagarjuna and his spiritual sons have not explicitly distinguished "essence mantra" (snying po), "close essence mantra" (nye snying) and "root mantra" (rtsa sngags), however, according to Acharya Abhaya "essence mantra" consists of the seed syllables and the name mantras of the respective deities interjected with the three syllables (OM AH HUM). This stands well. With regard to the "close essence mantra" the Root Tantra states,"This inner most essence of the Supreme Ones is emanated from his own vajra body, speech and mind." Hence, VAJRADHRK and so forth, the bare name mantras, are said to be the "close essence mantra". OM AH HUM are said to be the ultimate essence (de kho na nyid kyi snying po) of all deities. The "root mantra" refers to the rosary mantras (phreng sngags) of the four consorts and the nine fierce protectors as mentioned in the Root Tantra and the same mantras of the remaining deities mentioned in other Tantras." (See Khedrup Rinpoche, opcit, p 405).

46. "...It reveals that at the time of emanating deities (from the heart) one does

not do so holding the pride of the individual deities. Rather one emanates the remaining deities holding the pride of Hatred Vajra (zhe sdang rdo rje). However, while generating the deities in the lotus (mandala) of the consort one must generate the pride of being each of them because...". (Khedrup Rinpoche, ibid, p-367).

47. "Meditating on an inestimable mansion purifies an impure environment. What this means is: it is not that practitioners can transform all this impure environment into the inestimable mansion by doing such a meditation but they do it in order to purify themselves of their potency to utilize the impure environment in the future and also to ripen their potency by the completion stage for enjoying the inestimable mansion of exalted wisdom." (Khedrup Rinpoche, opcit, p 123).

48. Shakyamuni Buddha, after attaining his enlightenment, revealed three activities (spyod pa gsum) for the benefit of others. For those who are inclined to the lower path Buddha revealed the activity (path) of non-attachment; for others who are inclined to the extensive path he revealed the activity of spiritual grounds and perfections and for still others who are especially inclined towards the profound he revealed the activity of passion/attachment. In light of this, 'consorting with a knowledge-woman' (rig ma 'du bya wa) accords with the aspect of the last activity. In other words, passionate people can attain enlightenment through their passion. (See Khedrup Rinpoche, opcit, pp-343-344).

49. In the Perfection Vehicle a practitioner has to cultivate calm abiding eliminating the five obstacles by the eight antidotes and progressing on the nine levels of mind. But in the four classes of Tantra, without the need to cultivate calm abiding specifically as in the Perfection Vehicle, the deity yoga itself culminates in calm abiding and later the union of calm abiding and special insight. "Meditation on the subtle drop is explained in both the Yoga and Highest Yoga Tantras. Taking this into account the *Bright Lamp* (sgron gsal) has explained the subtle drop in general. According to Acharya Shakyamitra when one sees signs indicating the stability of the mind on a subtle symbol one has accomplished physical and mental ecstasy and this has been explained in many vast treatises such as the *Five Levels (sa sde)* as the attainment of the fully characterized calm abiding. Thus, at that time one has accomplished the fully characterized calm abiding. For this reason, the above Tantras do not explain an attainment of calm abiding apart from the meditation on deity yoga." (See Khedrup Rinpoche, opcit, p 394). "Having attained calm abiding there arises conventional special insight (ji snyed pa'i lhag mthong) with regard to emanating and withdrawing deities and symbols. Having generated strong ascertainment of emptiness, when one absorbs totally into the ultimate (truth) there arises the fully characterized special insight focussed on the ultimate (ji lta wa la dmigs pa'i lhag mthong). At this point one attains the fully characterized

special union of calm abiding and special insight." (See Khedrup Rinpoche, opcit, p 395).

50. "...If one wants to generate the completion stage exactly as explained in Tantras, at first one must engage in completing the generation stage." (Khedrup Rinpoche's *An Ocean of Attainments of the Generation Stage*, p 31).

51. "... one must know the difference between blocking ordinary appearance to the mind and refuting the existence of ordinary appearance in reality." (Khedrup Rinpoche, opcit, p 103).

52. "The first and third yogas of the level of verbal isolation -the meditation on the mantra drop at the heart and the meditation on the substance drop at the sexual organ - are designated as verbal isolation but are not actual verbal isolation because they do not actually involve the association of the breath with certain syllables." (See Highest Yoga Tantra, Daniel Cozort, Snow Lion Publications, Ithaca, NY, USA, 1986, p 85).

53. See Daniel Cozort, opcit, p 87.

54. "As for the vajra recitation of the generation stage, it is a mental recitation (yid bdzlas) free of sound and not moving one's tongue and lips..." See Khedrup Rinpoche, opcit, p 401.

55. See Daniel Cozort, opcit, p 86.

56. See Daniel Cozort, opcit, p 88.

57. "Those who rely on real consorts (should) have fulfilled complete qualifications as laid down in Tantras and authentic works of realized masters, such as, both the (male and female) practitioners should have ascertained the ultimate view of emptiness through the power of reasoning, mastery over the sequence of the four types of bliss/joy and especially from what level the spontaneous wisdom arises. In the case of the generation stage practitioners, they must be able to retain the (sperm of) altruism (at the tip of the secret organ) by the power of meditating on PHAT and in the case of completion stage practitioners they must be able to retain it (the sperm) by the power of wind-energy with mastery in the functioning of the vitality and exertion of consort(s) and so forth." (Khedrup Rinpoche, ibid, p-353).

58. See *Death, Intermediate State and Rebirth* by Lati Rinpoche and Jeffrey Hopkins, pp 38-42.

59. The twenty five coarse objects which dissolve at death are: the five physical and mental aggregates, the four elements, the six sources, the five objects and the five wisdoms.

60. "The meaning clear light of the completion stage is the source of all the deities of the states of union. And here, one dissolves (the deities of) "instantaneous generation" (lhag mos) into the clear light, which is the ultimate truth body of the generation stage, the source of all the deities from the Primordial Protector Complete Enjoyment Body to the Supreme Conqueror of the Mandala." (Khedrup Rinpoche, opcit, p 237).

61. "...even though there is no difference with regard to the (objective) emptiness that is meditated upon in both the Perfection Vehicle and the two stages - the generation and the completion (of Highest Yoga Tantra) - nonetheless there is a very great difference between the two vehicles in terms of the mode of meditation and the subjective mind which meditates (upon the objective emptiness) etc. And this must be understood." (Khedrup Rinpoche, opcit, p 101).

62. In this context a prior imagination of bliss and emptiness as non-dual on the generation stage is not just psyching oneself into a state, whether or not it has any real relation to the ultimate nature of things. Just as conceptual thinking of emptiness is essential to gain direct experience into it, similarly it is necessary to imagine bliss and emptiness as non-dual conceptually in order to experience their non-duality nature on the completion stage.

63. See *Death, Intermediate State and Rebirth*, Lati Rinpoche and Jeffrey Hopkins, p 30.

64. Ibid, pp 38-42.

65. See Other Related Works-15, 16 and 17.

66. See 3 Levels of the Kalachakra Stage of Completion, *Highest Yoga Tantra*, opcit, pp 123-128.